Feeding the Birds

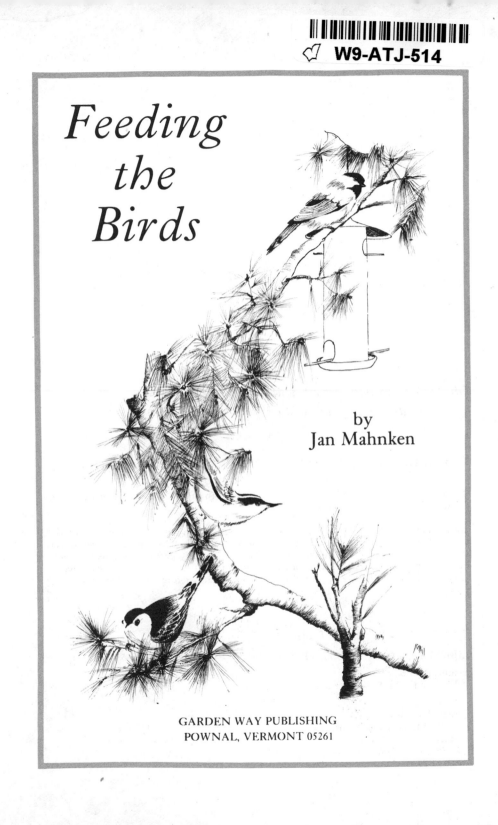

by
Jan Mahnken

GARDEN WAY PUBLISHING
POWNAL, VERMONT 05261

Illustrations by Kimberlee Knauf
Cover illustration by Elayne Sears

Printed in the United States

Printing (last digit): 10 9 8 7 6 5 4 3 2 1

LIBRARY OF CONGRESS CATALOGING IN PUBLICATION DATA

Mahnken, Jan.
  Feeding the birds.

  Bibliography: p.
  Includes index.
  1. Bird feeders. 2. Birds—Food. 3. Birds,
Attracting of. I. Title.
QL676.5.M333 1983   636.6   83-16365
ISBN 0-88266-361-5

Contents

For Bud, Bob, and Tom

1
Why
Feed the Birds?

Birds were not on the agenda for the day. We'd walked, conservatively, about a hundred miles. Times Square, through the Garment District, up Park Avenue to Grand Central Station, on to the United Nations. Studying our dog-eared map convinced us that taking a cab was the only sensible way to reach the American Museum of Natural History. Even so, by the time we spilled out of the big Checker, it was one o'clock, and we were starved.

We collapsed on benches in Central Park and gratefully addressed ourselves to the sandwiches we'd stuffed into our pockets earlier. The audience assembled quickly. In the foreground, pigeons bustled. On the fringes of their flock, several English sparrows skittered about. Starlings eyed us calculatingly. Nearer the trees, a couple of gray squirrels hovered. Tom crumbled a piece of crust and threw it towards the nearest pigeon. . . .

It happens all the time. Most people like to feed birds and animals, domestic or wild. When I was a child growing up in western Pennsylvania, I never ventured into Pittsburgh without sugar cubes in my pocket, in case I encountered one of the Black Horse Troop—and I took pains to insure encountering one of them. We and our children have fed squirrels and jays, sparrows and pigeons, swans, ducks, and geese (plus assorted stray dogs and cats) in parks everywhere we've traveled. At zoos, at sanctuaries, at various game farms, we've bought bread and peanuts and pellets from vending machines to feed to the featured inhabitants.

WIDE VARIETY

If anything, it's more fun to feed birds and animals around your own home. Wherever you live, you'll find a wide variety of wild life. Most of that variety comes in bird form. Worldwide, there are over 8,500 living bird species, 700 of them on our continent alone. Many are highly visible and relatively easy to attract if we provide food, water, and shelter.

Once embarked on the project of feeding the birds, you're likely to become more and more interested in them. Observing their behavior is easier because you've lured them into range. The beauty of the whole process is that it can be indulged in at whatever level appeals to you. It's a hobby you can begin with a minimum of fuss at any time of the year and continue at whatever rate you choose.

How do you begin? That's the easiest part of it. You don't actually even need a feeder. White bread broken into small pieces attracts birds. From that point on, it's a matter of refinement. Add a feeder. Provide water in a shallow, rough textured container. Put up some suet, buy some "bird" seed, and you're on your way.

It's as easy as that? Well, almost. Once you start, especially in lean times for the birds, there's the moral obligation to keep going, to be consistent. If birds learn to depend on your handouts, you ought to make sure that they continue to eat even if you're away from home. That can be arranged either through careful selection of food and feeders or through having someone else stock the feeders in your absence. Some people plan a feeding program that runs year-round; others supply food only when the natural supply is inadequate.

Don't forget that it's an expense—and even if you consider having an inordinate number of dependents a charity, the IRS doesn't. It must be admitted that there's another economic problem in attracting birds. They sometimes feed on crops intended for human or livestock consumption. We've planted a number of dwarf fruit trees in the side yard, and last year the robins consumed two-thirds of the cherry crop. (I gave the other cherry to Tom.) Catbirds take up summer residence in our raspberry patch, but fortunately there's enough produce to satisfy all of us. That seems to be the most effective way of dealing with bird depredations, at least on the individual level.

Probably the best reason to start feeding birds is that you *want* to start feeding birds. You enjoy having them around for a variety of reasons, mostly aesthetic. Their songs, their squawks, their comments drifting through the open windows on a summer day keep you informed of what's going on outside whether you can see it or not. Loafing on the porch steps after dinner, we watch the swallows darting about the pasture, the hummingbirds visiting petunias, the kingbird sitting motionless on a fence post. The evening grosbeaks, the cardinals, and the blue jays brighten up a winter day when the rest of the world seems somber in black and white and shades of gray.

STIMULATING HOBBY

There are other reasonable excuses to justify the trouble and expense that eventually accrue. Most of us are willing to invest time and money in a hobby strictly for our own pleasure. That's not enough? Well, there's no question of the potential for learning new things if you feed birds as a hobby. Developing a new interest is always pleasant and stimulating. When we were visiting my parents in Florida, one of their neighbors arranged a birding expedition for us. We saw unfamiliar birds in habitats we could never have discovered for ourselves in such short order. In addition, we had the pleasure of making new friends through our common interest.

You may discover that learning about birds has a few surprising ramifications. While reading a complicated suspense novel set in New York City, I came across a reference to a red-winged blackbird. The scene was Central Park, the time winter. That seemed odd. What was a red-winged blackbird doing in Central Park in the middle of winter? It's true they sometimes spend winters as far north as the Great Lakes and southern New England—occasionally. There was only that one reference to the bird: *the only bird in the entire book.* I became vaguely uncomfortable, wishing that the writer had not introduced the bird, or else had gone into greater detail. Was it merely a careless reference or did it have some symbolic significance? Based on an inadequate sampling of friends I've questioned, I'd be willing to bet that most readers raced past that bird with never a second thought. But it would be interesting to know how many bird lovers temporarily lost their way, like me, in the convoluted plot.

PRACTICAL BENEFITS

If your conscience demands practical reasons for attracting birds, consider their usefulness in reducing insect populations. Those starlings parading around the lawn will eat Japanese beetle larvae. Not only that, their beaks probing the ground for breakfast pick up and spread spores of a disease that helps control the beetles. The often maligned starling also goes after gypsy moth larvae, a delicacy scorned by most of the native birds. A northern (Baltimore) oriole consumes seventeen hairy caterpillars a minute,

The American goldfinch loves thistles.

and a pair of flickers will polish off 5,000 ants as a first course. Even birds that are primarily seed eaters feed their nestlings a diet high in insects.

Their appetite for fresh fruit in season may compete with ours, but we're surely willing to allow the birds to harvest the berries of poison ivy and sumac and the seeds of weeds. If it weren't for the American goldfinch, we'd be up to our hips in thistles and catnip. There's another angle to consider. By various means birds do a fine job of planting trees, shrubs, and other kinds of vegetation. People often find rather remarkable plants growing under their bird feeders. The birds have done their part in replacing the hedgerows that disappeared as a result of our passion for clean cultivation. The jay who buries an acorn and forgets where he cached it has helped to propagate oaks. To a certain extent, the birds thus help to maintain their own food supply and that of other animals. At the same time, they reduce soil erosion.

FUN FOR CHILDREN

You need still more ammunition to defend your pastime? Consider the children—your own or any you might be able to rope into the project. Our boys have shared in building feeders and birdhouses. They've helped keep them filled. They've scrambled up ladders to replace nestlings and decorated improvised hospitals with greenery in an effort to keep the patients comfortable. A black swan at Bok Tower instilled respect in Bob by a well-placed peck, and an incapacitated hummingbird taught Tom that transistors aren't the only astonishingly complex items to be found in small packages. First-hand experience sensitizes a child to the needs and demands of living creatures as watching Captain Kangaroo never could.

Because feeding birds brings them near enough to observe at close range, it can add another dimension to the lives of people whose horizons are necessarily limited. Radio and television have been boons to people confined indoors because of age, illness, or handicaps. They can't hold a candle to the pleasures of observing live creatures right outside the window. I'll never forget how my maternal grandmother enjoyed watching the birds that came to Mum's feeders on the front porch. Their antics occupied her during long hours as she recuperated from a broken hip.

CATS AREN'T A PROBLEM

Fine, you say, but I have this cat. . . . Don't worry. We have four. Our neighbors across the road have six. The area is crawling with cats—and birds. Well-fed domestic cats are not a major problem. Certain precautions should be taken, but the birds themselves take care of most situations that arise. I've seen them molesting and teasing the cats more frequently than the reverse.

The clinching argument for feeding birds? I think we have a responsibility to them. We've interfered extensively with their environment as our population has expanded. It's quite true that the extinction of species occurs naturally; man's interference, however, has accelerated the rates alarmingly. We owe them. It's a debt that can be paid in part by making our property more hospitable to birds.

2
The
Initial Plunge

I've mentioned that you can start a bird feeding program at any time of the year, and that's perfectly true. It's also true that, at least in some parts of the country, you'll get off to a more auspicious start in some seasons than in others.

In the middle tier of states, north to the latitude in which Massachusetts is the easternmost state, bird feeders get the least business from around the middle of August until late in October. Natural food supplies are abundant at that time. Migratory birds are beginning to get into the mood for setting out on the road and are restless. If the notion of catering to the birds strikes you during that slack period, October 1 is a good arbitrary date for beginning. Start a month earlier in the northernmost tier of states. The presence of even a few birds at that time may direct transient visitors to your feeder during migration and signal to winter residents as well. Because there isn't much turnover in resident birds in the deep South, Texas, and the Southwest, timing is less critical in those areas.

MIGRATIONS

We tend to become very much aware of birds during their spring and fall migrations because they gather in flocks and become highly visible and audible. The fall migration from north to south lasts more than twice as long as the spring one in the other direction. Along the shore it may begin in July. It will end sometime in November with the departure of finches and sparrows.

City folk can observe the migrations as easily as suburban and rural dwellers. As a matter of fact, the city is apt to be an especially good place to observe migration, because the small green yards amidst great expanses of concrete and asphalt are havens that can attract large numbers of migrants. Bird watchers in places such as Central Park in New York City may well see more species than do their country counterparts.

Most small land birds migrate by night, and they prefer clear nights with northerly winds. Controlled experiments with many species indicate that they use the stars as navigational aids. Foggy weather or heavy overcast and unfavorable breezes can lead them far off course. They may sometimes be seen going in the wrong direction until the weather clears and they're able to reorient themselves. Birds unusual to a given area occasionally come to feeders there because of navigational errors.

Migration, spring or fall, is not to be confused with mere wandering, which takes place at any season. Some birds travel great distances during the course of a season to follow a favored food supply. The failure of a crop may send them packing. But because birds of different species have varying food preferences, the failure of any *one* given crop isn't likely to cause the disappearance of all birds from that area. Some birds—the cardinal is a prime example, but goldfinches and purple finches are known to engage in the activity too—just seem to wander on a whim for no discernible rea-

son. We've become aware of these vagaries through the procedure of bird-banding, which enables ornithologists to keep track of the whereabouts of individual birds within a species.

Normally, the spring migration lasts only about two months. Perhaps not surprisingly, the first birds to return are those that traveled the least distance. Day length seems to trigger migration. Main-

taining a feeding station does not usually tempt migratory birds to refrain from their normal travel, although it may permit the survival of those members of a migratory species that for some reason (injury perhaps) were unable to leave with their cohorts. And there is evidence that the proliferation of feeding stations has extended the range boundaries of some species.

Because of the plethora of natural foods available, fall may be a slack time at many feeding stations despite the hordes of migrants passing through an area. If birds elect to stop in your yard, it's entirely possible that water, instead, will be the principal attraction. Nevertheless, keeping the feeder stocked, even for a small coterie of birds, is a good idea. The presence of this faithful nucleus is likely to attract other birds later on.

In contrast to the southern migration, those birds making their way north in spring are quite apt to visit feeding stations, because early in the season natural foods are at their lowest point. Other periods of heavy use occur during the winter months after a sudden drop in temperature or during snowstorms and periods of heavy snowcover.

ATTRACTING BIRDS

How will the birds know you've elected to become their patron?
The white foods, such as suet and white bread, seem to attract
their attention first. And it's primarily the scavengers—gulls, pigeons, starlings, grackles, house sparrows—who are first at the
scene of a brand new food supply. Who discovers your bird feeder
first will depend on the season and your location. The often-
despised house sparrows may well lead the way, though they are
primarily ground feeders. In most areas, these birds are no longer
so numerous that they prove a plague. Because they often serve as
guides for less aggressive birds (and because of their formidable
appetite for Japanese beetles), try not to think too harshly of
them.

If you have trees nearby, the jays and chickadees will be quick
to discover your feeder too. Jays have been observed sizing up the
situation at fast food restaurants, where scraps are often found, if
there is cover nearby. Cover is an important aspect of attracting

*Chickadee, chipping sparrow,
and titmouse appreciate good
cover.*

birds to your premises. Indeed, I find one of the more engaging characteristics of birds is their scorn for absolutely immaculate yards. They consider your brush pile, the briar patch, and the tangle of weeds behind the garage totally irresistible. If you can provide some trees and shrubbery, so much the better. Birds are an ornament more common to a yard that is less than spic and span.

We more often think about feeding birds in cold weather when their needs are more obvious. It's fuel that keeps them warm, and food provides that fuel. They're less likely to freeze to death if there is a certain amount of shelter from the weather (evergreens are especially useful to them) and plentiful food.

DON'T STOP TOO EARLY

There are arguments pro and con about feeding on a year-round basis. If you elect to stop with the return of mild weather, make sure you aren't too precipitate. A couple of weeks after the usual time of the last snowstorms or last average frost is a good target date.

You've decided to begin. You want birds in your yard, and the average city or suburban lot simply doesn't provide enough natural food to support many birds. Birds have enormous appetites relative to their size. East of the Mississippi River, for example, an acre of land will support only one to ten birds, and the average is four. It stands to reason, given the figures, that there's not going to be much bird activity in areas of dense human population without the help of those humans.

You just happen to have some leftover bread. You've eliminated the driveway and the walks as possible sites for the banquet since vehicles and pedestrians make those areas inappropriate except for occasional gestures. Where to serve the feast? What are the possibilities?

Remember that most of the birds attracted to feeders are primarily seed and/or insect eaters. Birds, whose eyes are proportionately larger than the eyes of most mammals, have superb vision. Experimental studies have compiled considerable evidence to indicate that they are attracted to white foods such as suet or white bread. These foods are therefore effective in introducing a new feeding area to birds. Although you may attract them originally with crumbs of white bread, cake, or doughnuts—birds seem to have the same depraved appetites as the rest of us—to keep them happy and healthy, you'll need to add something more substantial.

Seeds are available in blended mixtures or separately. Five pounds of blended seed called "wild bird food" will run about $1.50 to $2.50, depending on the components of the mix. Sunflower seeds cost more. Beef suet substitutes for the insects and can be fed straight from the butcher shop or in a cake made from rendered suet, with seeds added. You can whip them up yourself in the kitchen or buy them ready-made where you get your seed.

We'll go into more detail about specific foods for specific birds later on. Do remember that wet feed can become moldy and infect birds that eat it with the deadly fungus *Aspergillus fumigatus*. Clean feeders regularly. It's recommended that they be scrubbed and sprayed with a product such as Lysol. I confess that I know no one who does that. If uneaten food is removed, perhaps fresh air and sunshine do the trick of sanitizing. In any case, though thorough scrubbing may be the right way to go about it, the people with whom I'm acquainted (and, admittedly, myself) do not follow this recommended practice.

Supplied with your bird groceries, your next step is to dispense them. Before rushing out to buy the avian equivalent of The Coach House, you might consider a few alternatives. Look around your residence. The flat roof of our side porch is accessible from the guest room windows and provides a wide flat expanse on which birds could feed comfortably, and we could see them easily. It struck me as a great possibility for bird feeding. There was just one hitch. The roof was the favorite sunbathing area for our cats, at all seasons. If you have such an area and it happens to be inaccessible to felines, it might be just the ticket.

ARGUMENTS AGAINST CATS

Cats are the first predators that come to mind when we talk of songbirds in the garden. Few people are indifferent to cats. You like 'em or you don't. I happen to belong in the first category, and my attitudes reflect that. Despite what their detractors say, cats are not evil. They are simply cats. It's as pointless to blame them

for stalking birds as it is to praise them for catching mice or rats or other four-footed beasts you want to eliminate. In some books on the subject I've studied, I've encountered some really remarkable ways of dealing with the cat situation.

Most contemporary writers seem reasonable (though the argument rumbles on, as witness letters to *Audubon*), but some of the earlier ones became all but incoherent when discussing cat problems. In one widely known work, Ernest Harold Baynes (*Wild Bird Guests*. New York: E.P. Dutton, 1915) suggests that anyone who keeps such a creature as a pet (and has, presumably, grown fond of it, for inexplicable reasons) ought to resolve never to acquire another once it dies. He seemed to consider the action a moral obligation, if not a penance for the original sin of keeping a cat. Baynes considered cats almost entirely lacking in merit and terrible carriers of diseases, such as bubonic plague, diphtheria, and tuberculosis.

One writer recommends the use of a "cat-proof" fence around your property. It should be six feet high and angled outwards at the top another two feet so cats can't climb in. Quite aside from its appearance, one can imagine the prohibitive expense of such an item, even for a small lot.

An English writer (C. Percival Staples. *Birds in a Garden Sanctuary*. London and New York: Frederick Warne and Co., Ltd., 1946) sensibly remarks, "The cat-proof fence has yet to be invented and is a very unlikely benefaction of the future." He suggests that keeping a dog on the premises is likely to be effective in making an area unattractive to cats. Other writers suggest shooting cats, poisoning them, or trapping them. It is true that they admit that a modicum of tact should be used when coping with the neighbors' cats, but it's clear that they're all in favor of eradicating the pests.

Another more sympathetic writer proposes politely asking your neighbors to "bell" their cats. The sound of the bell, attached to cats' collars, alerts birds to their presence. That sounds like a reasonable suggestion, though fledglings (which are particularly vulnerable) are unlikely to perceive a tinkling bell as a warning. It might help adult birds in some areas—civilized areas, with fairly sedentary cats. The collars, naturally, must be the safety-type which break open if the cat gets entangled in something, or they will be highly effective traps all by themselves. In our neighborhood, a rural one, such a collar has a life expectancy of approximately twelve hours, since they break easily.

Dedicated cat-lovers though we are, we don't want our pets, or the pets of our neighbors, killing the songbirds. The birds themselves take certain precautions. So do we. They seem highly effective.

PRECAUTIONS

For a start, our free-standing feeders are mounted on one-inch galvanized pipe driven into the ground. We adopted this tactic because a couple of our cats took to having their mid-day siestas *in* the feeder trays when the feeders were mounted on stout wooden posts. This was a danger to the birds only in that it prevented their feeding for long periods.

Our suspended feeders are carefully placed so that cats can't ambush the birds. We use branches only if cats can't get above them. Ground feeding is conducted only in open areas and the water is out in the open too so the cats can't lie hiding nearby.

There are suitable trees and shrubs close enough where the birds can preen. Whenever we notice fledglings just out of the nest, we bring the cats *and* dogs indoors because fledglings are easy prey.

If the parent birds are in evidence, you can bet the cats won't be. I've seen our pets racing for cover, pursued by irate barn swallows, the cats loudly protesting their innocence all the time they're retreating. The birds, by the way, won't bother a sleeping cat.

If you have no cats and/or prefer not to have any others in your yard, "whoosh" them. They'll leave. Cats are, by nature and conditioning, careful to avoid areas where they're unwelcome. If your locale is plagued with feral cats, as opposed to well-fed domestic cats, notify your game warden. It's also both sensible and humane to neuter cats not needed for breeding purposes. It will help prevent the high incidence of strays and feral cats.

PREDATOR BIRDS

Cats, of course, aren't the only predators of birds. Birds themselves prey on other birds. At one time hawks and other birds of prey were shot on sight. Baynes and other writers earlier in this century report, with undisguised glee, their success in killing birds of prey. Fortunately, a more reasonable attitude now prevails. Recently we observed a pigeon hawk strike a robin right outside our kitchen window, on a broad expanse of lawn. Yes, we were saddened at the loss of the robin. But I confess to a keen interest in the event too. We can—and should—protect birds from danger that *we* introduce into their environment, but let's not go monkeying around with natural enemies. Hummingbirds sometimes get caught in spider webs when they're collecting nesting materials. They're occasionally swallowed by bass or bullfrogs while drinking. One birder reported seeing a hummingbird fall victim to a praying mantis! There's no need to interfere. It's all part of the food chain. Without checks on their numbers, our songbirds would run out of their food supplies.

SENTINEL BIRDS

Birds themselves have their own methods of coping with predators. The often-maligned jays act as sentinels, calling the attention of other birds to all manner of intruders, hawks and shrikes as well as cats and other mammals. Jays and other birds use a variety of alarm calls, depending on whether the enemy is approaching by air or on the ground. Open country birds tend to be more "flighty" than woodland birds because their environment offers

them less protection. Evidence suggests that brightly colored birds are less palatable than those with dull plumage. The latter often "freeze" when alarmed. Birds can often be seen ganging up on or "mobbing" their enemies, a tactic which frequently drives the enemy away. Usually such attacks are all bluff, but birds have been known to kill snakes. Several different species may cooperate in mobbing.

If you take reasonable care and don't set the birds up, those at your feeders aren't in dreadful peril. Contemporary writers generally believe that depredations by hawks and cats are minor and usually involve the aged, crippled, or diseased birds.

SQUIRRELS

Probably the most common pests at feeding stations are the squirrels. The ingenuity invested in foiling squirrels has been truly prodigious. Even if you don't object to supporting them, their presence at a feeder prevents the birds from eating, often for dangerously long periods. Squirrels have become problems at urban and suburban feeders because they adapt more easily to densely populated areas than do their enemies, so they've increased their numbers greatly. The devices available to thwart their attempts to use bird feeding stations are numerous. If you buy a feeder for birds, it's relatively easy to get a "squirrel-proof" one. They will be discussed in more detail in the following chapter. For homemade or non-squirrel-proof feeders, a few commonsense precautions will keep the situation under control.

Keep feeders at least eight feet from trees, fences, or buildings from which squirrels can jump to their dinner. Free-standing feeders on pipe will discourage squirrels from climbing. Posts can be greased or wooden posts sheathed in metal. Metal cones mounted

Metal cone will defeat the hungriest squirrel.

underneath feeders will prevent the creatures from climbing up. Many, though not all, of the deterrents for cats will be effective for squirrels too.

We once had a trolley feeder on a clothesline. The squirrels nimbly walked the rope from the tree to which it was attached at one end. In desperation, my husband finally took a shot at one of the marauders, which quite effectively solved the problem. He missed the squirrel, but hit the feeder dead center. I have since heard that the problem can be solved by putting lengths of derelict plastic hose over the rope on either side of the trolley feeder so the squirrel's feet have no purchase. It's not as colorful a solution, perhaps, but reportedly more satisfactory. If you enjoy feeding the squirrels, put their food—corn or whatever—in a separate area.

Chipmunks, rats, mice, and raccoons may also be attracted to your feeding station, but they're considerably more easily discouraged than squirrels because they're not as agile. Action you take to prevent squirrels from gobbling all the goodies will prevent these other animals from becoming much of a nuisance.

SIMPLE FEEDERS

Margaret Millar, in her delightful book, *The Birds and Beasts Were There* (New York: Random House, 1967), started her feeding program on a wide ledge outside the living room windows. Such simple beginnings have much to recommend them, especially to those of us who are indolent and/or prone to procrastination. They are readily stocked and they bring the birds close enough to be enjoyed. Their limitations, unfortunately, are pronounced. To begin with, many houses don't have such convenient architectural attributes. There's also the problem of untidiness, which involves not only aesthetic but also sanitary considerations. The mess has to be cleaned up periodically. And make no mistake, birds are terrifically messy. (Ever see the havoc a budgie—*one* budgie can create in a room?) The greater your success in attracting visitors, the more frequent and arduous your housekeeping chores.

With any feeding area adjacent to windows, you must also consider the problem of birds smashing into the glass. Owl or other predator silhouettes, sold for the purpose of preventing such calamities, will just as effectively prevent birds enjoying the feast you've provided, so you've got to think of some other solution. Screens remaining in place outside the window may work in some cases; sheer curtains which prevent the birds from considering the window a flying area may be even better. They have the extra advantage of masking *you* and giving you a better chance of observing your guests close up.

In addition, even if cats can't find their way to the area, rats, mice, squirrels, raccoons, and snakes (which feed on the mice!) just may. Cats and squirrels are problems enough; most of us aren't prepared to support the entire wild population of our neck of the woods.

BIRD TABLE

The bird table, a near relative of the ledge-roof approach, has many of its virtues as well as its disadvantages. It need not be designed for the purpose, though it may be; any table impervious to weather will serve. It will accommodate significant numbers of birds and, since tables are portable, its location can minimize some of the problems associated with feeding the creatures actually *on* the house. Because it may be placed at some distance from the house, shyer species may be attracted, and you're less likely to have birds banging into windows. Keeping it tidy is usually easier than policing ledges and roofs but remains a necessary task.

MAKE IT YOURSELF

Before rushing out to buy a feeder, take stock of the basement or barn or shed or garage. There must be *something* there with which to fashion a feeder. Even the constitutionally inept (our category) can produce a satisfactory one with a minimum of effort and expense.

If you have the time, interest, and requisite carpentry skills, you can read many books that give detailed instructions for making handsome feeders, from garden variety to sumptuously sophisticated. Walter E. Schutz's *Bird Watching, Housing and Feeding* (Milwaukee: The Bruce Publishing Co., 1963), later published in a revised edition under the title *How to Attract, House and Feed Birds* (New York: Bruce, 1970), is one of many that will be useful to those with the ability and inclination to build more complicated structures.

Remember to coat the outside of the feeder with a stain, but leave the interior bare. Birds prefer the dullness of the stain to the brightness of paint; a natural finish is less threatening to them.

BOARD FEEDER

The simplest feeder I've seen described is nothing more than a board, preferably with a rim(the better to keep the feed from blowing or sliding off), attached to a windowsill. Dimensions, of course, are determined by the size of the window chosen.

Another simple feeder is made from a coconut. Remove the milk and saw the coconut lengthwise in half. Leave the meat inside as a treat, if you like. Drill three holes through which to thread wire or stout twine, near the sawed part, so that it can be hung like a hanging pot. Fill with seed, bacon grease, and peanut butter or other delicacies, and *voilà*, an instant feeder, ready to go. Two instant feeders, even.

There is considerable evidence to suggest that a simple open tray-type feeder, similar to the bird table but mounted about five feet from ground level, may be the most effective way to attract birds. Since the food will be unprotected from snow and rain, the tray should have drainage holes drilled in it. Whatever food drops through these holes will be eaten by birds that prefer to feed on the ground. Absence of a roof makes the food more visible to passing birds, and it prevents the more cautious of them, who may at first be suspicious of closed-in places, from being spooked. If birds seem reluctant to feed close to the house, the feeders can first be placed at some distance and gradually moved closer. If feeding from windowsills is your eventual goal, a trolley feeder is especially useful. Every couple of days you can inch it a bit closer to the house. The food will remain in approximately the same location, so the birds will have no difficulty in finding it.

FEEDER KITS

Some stores offer feeder kits for about $7. These are easily put together. Youngsters just beginning to be interested in birds and/or building may be pleased with such a project. With the kit they can put together a good-looking feeder with few problems.

Another type of feeder, dear to the hearts of den mothers and scoutmasters, is the length of log with holes drilled in it. Usually the bark is left on, the better for bird feet to maintain a grip and also, I suspect, to make it look suitably rustic and unobtrusive. Most of these logs have a screw eye attached to one end so they can be hung from a branch. Fancier models provide perches at the drilled holes. Schutz gives instructions, in fact, for versions so complicated to make that they would delight a dedicated woodworker.

This feeder doubles as a suet dispenser and as a grease-concoction dispenser. You can mix peanut butter with partially hardened bacon grease and perhaps some birdseed or cornmeal and push the mixture into the holes. This is easier said than done. Please note that this is, of necessity, a cold weather procedure. In my experience, this particular feeder needs refilling by the time you get indoors, remove your boots, and hang up your coat. Children, however, seem to love it. At least, they love to make them.

When requested to fill them, they remember urgent business else-where or tell you they have too much homework.

The biggest selection of commercial bird-feeding equipment is found in most retail outlets in the fall, but some is available year-round. My own favorite garden center stocks a bewildering assort-ment of feeding stations. They tell me that their biggest seller is a small feeder made by Duncraft called the "e-z fill." Its modest price—around $4—makes it attractive to beginners who aren't sure just how involved they want to get in this business. We'll consider other available kinds, including specialized feeders, in the next chapter.

GROUND FEEDING

Don't neglect the ground itself as a feeding area. Some birds are reluctant to feed anywhere else. Spills from the other feeding equipment you use often provide enough food to satisfy ground feeders. If that approach seems inadequate for your particular crowd, choose an area with cover nearby. In soggy or snowy weather, a canvas tarpaulin or a piece of plywood can be used to minimize waste of food. Surfaces such as these can—and should—be cleaned regularly to maintain hygienic conditions and to re-main visually possible to cope with. So few of us are prepared to go to these lengths that the birds who prefer to eat on the ground are more often left to their own devices in scrounging what they can from feeder overflow.

Okay. You've got the basics. Now you have to decide where to put them. There are several considerations to keep in mind. You want to be able to see the birds from indoors. The feeders should be in a protected location and near cover for the birds. On the other hand, you want them to be easy to reach for stocking. In areas of heavy snowfall, this can be a real problem. That feeder, so conveniently located beside the driveway or front walk, suddenly has a high wall of snow separating you and it after the plow or the snowthrower gets finished clearing. If it's too close to areas that are plowed, it may actually be damaged by the snow-moving equipment. Moreover, those piles of snow may make the feeders suddenly accessible to animals you don't intend to feed, or to those that have designs on the birds. Try to make sure the feeder can be reached for cleaning and filling without the use of a step-ladder. There's nothing quite like a hassle of that nature to dampen your enthusiasm for the whole business, especially in inclement weather.

The population at the feeder will vary somewhat from season to season, and actual numbers may not remain constant.

Although opinions differ on the amounts of food that will be consumed at different times of the year, a surprising number of people insist that they fill their feeders on a regular schedule, at a constant rate, and find little or no difference in the amount they use at different seasons. Perhaps that phenomenon results from somewhat less dependence from a larger population of birds in times of natural abundance and greater dependence from a smaller population in times of natural scarcity. Or maybe it's that more people stock stations in cold weather and the birds distribute themselves over a wider area and visit multiple feeders.

3
Bird
Feeders and Food

Two different sets of circumstances may prompt you to expand your feeding program. Perhaps you have had such success in attracting birds that they're all but standing in line to partake of the banquet. On the other hand, maybe you haven't been able to attract some of the birds you especially want in your yard. In the first case you simply need more feeders. In the second, you may need different kinds of feeders or a different menu.

Overcrowding at feeders leads to all sorts of difficulties. Some of the birds will fight among themselves. Starlings and many other birds will drive the less aggressive of their own and other species away. It's hardly a surprising phenomenon and is common in other animals, including man. Too many equals stress.

You've heard of "pecking order" in chickens. The boss chicken pecks everyone below her, and all the other chickens have a specified place in the scheme, dominant to the chickens farther down the line, subordinate to those above. Wild birds don't have conditions as stable as those of domestic chickens, so you'll find among them a "peck dominance" instead, depending on the situation at the time. There will always be a certain amount of friction, but it can be minimized by having a variety of foods and feeders available to your guests. A single species or individual can't then dominate so easily.

FEEDING TOGETHER

Many kinds of birds feed together quite amicably. Doves and woodpeckers and chickadees, for example, won't squabble. But they prefer different foods, different methods. Understanding their preferences will enable you to exclude or minimize "undesirables," such as starlings and sparrows, in your bird feeders. Varying locations will also appeal to different species.

Birds that prefer ground feeding include juncos, sparrows, doves, quail, cardinals, jays, starlings, towhees, and thrashers. Some of them (but not quail and doves) will fly to a platform feeder to get food but take it elsewhere to eat it. Swinging feeders discourage jays and house sparrows but will attract cardinals, chickadees, finches, nuthatches, and titmice. Let's examine some of the ready-built feeder types available. Do-it-yourselfers can build similar feeders.

TUBULAR FEEDERS

The best feeders conserve feed, are available in all kinds of
weather, and are safe from disturbances, including predators.
These are some of the reasons that tubular feeders have become
very popular in recent years. Several manufacturers supply similar
models. One made in Minnesota is called "The Bird Tree." "Droll
Yankee" is made in Rhode Island, and so are "K-feeders." Aspects
offers a square tubular model with a white cedar roof. Duncraft in
New Hampshire also has a line of tubular feeders.

Some of these companies have complete lines, ranging in price
from $5 or $6 to $70, and still rising, depending on capacity,
amenities, and the growing sophistication of the feeders. Some use
only metal fittings, and their prices reflect this, starting higher.
Some feeders must be hung; others have a pipe thread built into
the bottom for post mounting. The tube itself is constructed of
clear plastic and has perches at the feeding stations. It's easy to see
when refilling is in order, and the feed is protected from rain or
snow.

Tubular feeders are designed to hold and dispense either thistle
or sunflower seeds. The latter kind will also handle cracked corn
or a mix of wild bird seeds. The least expensive ones are hanging
models sixteen inches long and two inches in diameter with two
perches and feeding ports near the bottom of the tube. At the
same price you can buy eight-inch prefilled models.

In a kind of mid-price range, from $8 to $15, you'll find tubular
feeders with from four to eight feeding stations, each with a
wooden perch. If you want brackets from which to hang the
tubes, you'll need another $3 to $4. They're made of clear acrylic,
are about ten inches long, and support up to fifteen pounds. They
mount, with screws, to post, tree, or window. Some are equipped
with four perches for birds waiting their turn at the feeder. For
still another $4, you can lock a "high impact polystyrene" seed
tray, in a metallic finish, to the bottom of one line of tubular feeders to accommodate still more eager eaters.

Add $3 for a sixteen-inch diameter squirrel guard which "prop-
erly installed makes any hanging feeder squirrel-proof." A "tilt-
top" baffle that "works every time!" is made of clear plastic and

Birds quickly learn to use tubular feeders.

has its own hardware for suspending a feeder. It's the same size as the other one but more sophisticated, and costs $17.50. Some of the top-of-the-line tubular feeders, starting at around $15, are advertised as squirrel-proof anyway. They have a metal cap and base, and some have metal perches with insulated perch guards. (Squirrels may *eat* wooden perches.) Songbirds are afraid of squirrels and keep their distance if the squirrels have access to feeders. In urban areas, shy on hawks, owls, and human hunters, squirrels can be a colossal nuisance to people trying to feed birds. Hence the emphasis on deterring them.

Several models of tubular feeders have metal baffles within and metal reinforcing around the feeding ports themselves to prevent waste and spilling. Some of the feeders in this $15 price range will hold four pounds of thistle seed, which is a *lot* of thistle seed. But if you want a feeder that large (twenty-four inches) and also squirrel-proof, be prepared for another price hike, up to $20 or more. The most complicated one I've seen will dispense sunflower, thistle, and mixed seed independently and simultaneously. It has a seven- to nine-pound capacity, nine feeding stations, a seed tray, and a squirrel guard. *That's* deluxe. It costs around $25.

FEEDER POSTS

You like the idea of mounting a tubular feeder on a post? Such a post is available. It will fit any flat-bottomed wooden post feeders and, with adaptors, some of the tubular feeders as well. It comes equipped with a movable plastic sleeve at the top which dumps squirrels to the ground and automatically returns to the top of the pole. All yours, for $18.

Besides the tubular feeders, there are others designed to be hung. One, made of nylon netting, is used to dispense thistle. Called a "thistle stocking," it is twelve inches long and holds twelve ounces of thistle. It retails for about $3. The birds love it, but do remember that it doesn't protect from weather the way the tubular feeders do. For around $4, there's the "e-z fill," mentioned in the previous chapter. It is an eight-inch clear plastic cylinder, filled by rotating the roof, which rests on a six-inch feeding tray. Up around $5 you'll find the "beehive" type, made of polyethylene in "warm burnt sienna brown." It's designed to hold sunflower seeds for the small birds that will cling to a feeder, such as chickadees, nuthatches, and finches.

SMALL BIRDS SPECIAL

Also for the small birds is the "satellite" feeder, advertised as spillproof, leakproof, and big-bird proof. It's six inches in diameter and sells for around $9. For $20 you can buy a feeder with frost-free wire fencing which permits only small birds to enter. A small version goes for $13. Both can be suspended or post mounted. For close to $30, a feeder bowl comes equipped with the "tilt-top" squirrel guard previously described.

The variety of feeders available is surprising. Want to cater to cardinals and other birds of similar size? There's a special feeder for them, for $18, to be mounted or hung. A hanging feeder for thistle with cone-shaped roof and "feed-saving slots" for the birds runs $6. "A-frame" feeders are hung through the highest part of the roof in order to make them squirrel-proof and go for about $10 to $12. Tray-type feeders, to be suspended or post-mounted, run anywhere from $4 for tiny ones up to around $15 for larger ones. All but the least expensive have a central hopper of clear plastic to dispense the seed. Depending on its size, you might be able to stock it with a supply lasting several days. A few hopper types are available in kit form, starting at $7.

Some hanging feeders are equipped with weathervanes and have only one open side. They turn with the wind, protecting both birds and feed. Try mounting a suspended feeder on a trolley instead of hanging it from a fixed point. It makes for ease of stocking in inclement weather, and it's a splendid way to lure the birds gradually closer and closer to viewers.

WINDOWPANE FEEDERS

Windowpane feeders, made mostly or entirely of clear acrylic, are prized even above trolley feeders for their ease of filling and for bringing birds really close to observers. Most are held to the window by transparent suction cups, which lift free for filling the feeder. They range from 3½ inches to over 20 inches in size, from $7 to $15. One windowpane feeder is made specifically for dispensing thistle. Another, for $12, is designed to hold suet.

SUET HOLDERS

Ways of offering suet are nearly as varied as methods of offering other bird foods. Some feeders have a special section at one end, a kind of basket arrangement, to hold it. Probably the simplest way to proceed is to put a chunk in a mesh onion bag and hang it up, suspended from a tree or the branch of a sturdy shrub or some protruding part of the house, garage, or whatever. The fact that it swings will, however, discourage some of the visitors you may want to attract. An alternative is to nail it fast to a convenient surface.

Still relatively easy but more permanent (and less unsightly) a procedure is to fashion a container of heavy gauge wire. Some people suggest coating the wire with paraffin so various portions of bird anatomy don't stick to the wire in freezing weather. You have the option of hanging it or attaching it to a surface.

Many birds will enjoy this suet feeder.

Should you not have on hand the materials to make a suet-holder, you can buy one ready-made easily and nearly as inexpensively as buying the materials. Some are designed to be mounted on a tree or the side of a building, some to be suspended. Most are wire cages in various shapes and sizes, priced from $4 to $14. The more expensive ones have roofs to offer weather protection. Suet gets a lot of attention because it's considered a choice food by at least forty-five species of garden birds. Breads or fruits can be stashed in the holders as well as, or in addition to, suet.

If you think of a particular bird-feeding problem, chances are some manufacturer has come up with a solution for it. One feeder is made especially for bluebirds, with clear plastic sides and 1½-inch holes to exclude robins, mockingbirds, and other larger birds who might be tempted by the raisins and currants used to coax the bluebirds inside. It has a hinged roof for easy filling. Add sunflower seeds or nutmeats and the chickadees, titmice, and nuthatches will enter, too. In the South, you'll find quail feeders. Since they're placed on the ground, they have the disadvantage of attracting rabbits, squirrels, mice, rats, and snakes. The snakes are after the rats and mice, not the quail food.

HUMMINGBIRD FEEDERS

The greatest amount of attention given to the feeding of a single bird is that lavished on hummingbirds. It all started with simple tubes of sugar-water, a method originated by an enterprising amateur. Strips of red and orange ribbon attached to the tubes attracted the hummingbirds' attention. At some point, a birder trying to attract hummingbirds to a vial of sugar-water attached a flower to its neck. The hummingbirds were astonished at the quantities of nectar in that wondrous flower. Many ready-built feeders now come equipped with plastic flowers.

You can get started in the business of catering to hummingbirds—strictly a seasonal occupation except at our southernmost borders—for around $5. Your five-dollar bill will buy you a two-ounce feeder, a bee guard, and nectar. From there on, the sky's the limit. There's one "Nectar Bar" that attaches to a window. You can feed anywhere from one to eight birds with a single feeder holding from two ounces all the way up to a whopping sixty-four ounces. Some of them have canopies to shelter the birds from rain. The price range goes to around $30. If you feel the urge, add a $5

 wrought iron hanger, or, for $3, a sturdy hanging chain with a clamp that makes it easier to detach any hanging feeders for refilling.

A friend of mine in New Mexico, Donna Sierra, told me about a visit she made to friends who lived near the Gila River. They had hung out what Donna describes as an ordinary hummingbird feeder and had at least thirty hummingbirds around it all day long. They had to replenish it three or four times a day. Sometimes, by the way, other birds learn to use hummingbird feeders. Orioles have been observed refreshing themselves at the devices.

It's clear that you can spend remarkable amounts of money on bird feeders, if you choose to do so. It may be fun, but it isn't actually necessary. Homemade ones, whether aesthetically pleasing or merely serviceable, will be acceptable to the birds. They have less exacting standards than we do in such matters.

MUST BE FILLED

The main requirement is to keep those feeders filled once the birds discover them. Handy quart or gallon seed dispensers with tapered spouts are available, costing from $2.50 to $5. We make do with a coffee can. For $10 you can get a seed bucket, with carrying handle, which will store fifteen to twenty-five pounds of seed, depending on what kind it is. We store ours, usually in the sacks it's packaged in, in garbage cans in the barn. If you don't store bird feed in your house, you'll discover it's a good idea to use vermin-proof containers.

Some birds will be casualties in bad weather despite your best efforts. Either they don't come to the feeder at all, or there's not enough shelter. (We'll get to shelter you can provide for them in following chapters.) This thinning of the ranks is regarded by some ornithologists as nature's way of checking bird populations when a series of mild winters has prompted birds to overextend their normal ranges.

You'll observe what we consider thievery in birds at all seasons. Some birds are more apt to engage in the activity than others, perhaps because they're more competent in its pursuit. They raid caches made by other birds. Jays often carry food away and hide it, apparently for use in leaner times. They have been observed burying sunflower seeds, in neat rows, about a foot apart. The seeds sprouted. Now, if birds could only be taught to hoe. . . .

Hoarded foods are sometimes taken by watchful competitors. Among those who will steal food stored by other species are chickadees, house sparrows, grackles, starlings, brown thrashers, and sparrows. Some of the group will steal from each other too, often almost from the very beak of a feeding bird. House sparrows dart in and pluck food from in front of grackles. Considering that grackles frequently kill them—and sometimes other birds as well—with a swift blow to the head, this is a decidedly risky business. They never seem to learn that grackles have short fuses. The grackles, after dispatching their victims, either carry them off or devour their brains on the spot. Another distressing behavior, to be observed in times of really severe food shortages, is cannibalism among songbirds. Keep those feeders stocked!

Sometimes injured birds, including hawks, will visit feeders. At migration time, such birds may be unable to undertake a long journey. It's possible that your feeder will enable them to survive the winter. Other birds sometimes molest, sometimes shun injured or oddly colored birds (albinos, for example, are not uncommon). Most of them tend to ignore injured, hungry hawks at feeders, but grackles have been observed to heckle them.

THE MENU

Anyone who goes to the trouble of erecting multiple feeding stations for the birds is apt to decide to try different kinds of foods. Let's start with the kinds you buy just for the purpose. It's important to shop around for the best prices you can find, because they vary widely. If you live in an area handy to a livestock feed store, you'll discover that prices are almost invariably cheaper there than at "bird departments" in stores or garden centers. This is partly the result of buying in bulk, but there will even be variations from one feed store to another. My own source of supply is 30 to 100 percent cheaper on food items than is my favorite garden store, and 15 to 30 percent cheaper than some other feed stores.

THISTLE

I've mentioned thistle feeders, so we'll begin there. Thistle is expensive, running close to $2 a pound if bought in small quantities. The good news is that it's bulky, and most people who feed a variety of foods use only a few pounds of thistle a year. It goes a long way if it's fed from feeders designed for it.

Our friends the Wickwires, just up the road, stock five or six feeders with cracked corn, mixed wild birdseed, sunflower seed, and thistle year-round for a large number of birds. Though they use fifty pounds of sunflower seed in a little over a month (and correspondingly large amounts of the corn and mix), they tell me that ten pounds of thistle lasts them about a year. Their thistle feeder is kept full at all times; no rationing.

A certain economy is possible by buying in bulk. A twenty-five- pound bag costs around $40, and you might want to club together with other feeders of birds on such a costly item. Thistle is more properly called niger, which is a member of the thistle family, and is often sold under that name. The seed is imported from Africa, primarily Ethiopia. One of its advantages, mitigating its cost, is that it's impervious to wet weather. Among the birds that dote on thistle are finches, sparrows, chickadees, titmice, towhees, and juncos. Mourning doves like it, but they can't handle the thistle feeders. Considering their appetites, it's just as well.

SUNFLOWER SEEDS

Sunflower seed is another of the foods often fed separately. In small quantities, it costs about $.60 a pound, but it's popular with so many birds that it's not only more economical but more convenient to buy it in large quantities. A fifty-pound sack generally goes for $15, but my supplier sells it for $11.45. I told you it's worthwhile to shop around. Sunflower kernels (already shelled) are another matter. A five-pound bag sells for $5. It's less messy, perhaps, but close to prohibitive in price. Most people I've talked to who feed sunflower seeds separately use fifty pounds in six weeks, year-round. That is a considerable investment, and you may decide that if the birds want sunflower kernels, they can jolly well crack the seeds themselves. The many who are willing to do so include titmice, grosbeaks, chickadees, nuthatches, towhees, jays, cardinals, and blackbirds. Starlings and sparrows, which have difficulty cracking the seeds, are likely to pounce on bits and pieces left by birds with stronger beaks. If a flock of grosbeaks descends on your feeder, the sunflower seeds will disappear in short order. For one thing, grosbeaks usually arrive in flocks, not singly, and their appetites are prodigious. One observer reported seeing a single evening grosbeak consume ninety-six (he counted) sunflower seeds in five minutes. Better buy them in fifty-pound bags.

One item may puzzle you when you dispense sunflower seeds: they may not look like the ones you sow in your garden. There are two different kinds. The big striped ones that we grow are used for their showy flowers and for human confections. The much smaller black seeds usually sold for bird food are the kind that are pressed for oil.

If you feed sunflower seeds, you'll have large piles of hulls under the feeders in the spring. Don't toss these into the garden or compost pile. They have a substance that inhibits the growth of plants.

MIXES

The same feeders that dispense sunflower seeds will handle the mixtures sold as "wild bird food." These combinations vary widely in cost, depending on the proportions of ingredients and the size of the bag. The five-pound bags of seed available in supermarkets start at $1.50 and go up from there. Comparable mixes at feed stores and garden centers sell for $13 for fifty to 100 pounds. That's a big difference. A mixture containing 40 percent sunflower seeds costs $13 for twenty pounds.

What else besides sunflower seeds is in these mixes? Ingredients—and proportions—vary, but most contain some variety of millet, rape seed, sorghum, and canary seed. The advantages of a commercial mix are its convenience and appeal to a variety of birds.

Those who are so inclined can devise their own mixes, usually at lower cost, to appeal to particular species or in an effort to exclude "undesirable" birds. You'll probably have to resort to a feed store to get some of the ingredients. The only one of those seeds mentioned above that I've seen at a store stocking bird supplies was yellow proso millet, the tiny round seed that forms the base of many mixes. It was priced at $1.99 for three pounds, so high it wouldn't be practical to use it in your own mix. The procedure of formulating your own mix is so complicated that most of us who feed birds use a ready-made mix and feed special foods like thistle and sunflower seed separately. That eliminates finding a source for mix ingredients in bulk and also the need for storage space for them.

CRACKED CORN

In some stores that sell bird supplies, you'll find cracked corn, popular with a large number of birds, especially game birds. It sells at such places for $13 per fifty-pound bag. You'll save from 50 to over 100 percent by buying it at a feed store. One place I checked had it for $8.90 for a 100-pound bag. You pay a tremendous amount for the convenience of getting it in the smaller amounts at a wild bird supply department.

In roughly the same price category, at feed stores, you can buy scratch feed, a mixture of cracked corn and some other grain, usually wheat. It comes in three grades: fine, medium, and coarse. Choose according to the size bird you'd like to attract with it. There is one disadvantage to keep in mind when dispensing cracked corn or scratch feed: it spoils rather quickly in wet weather. You should dispose of feed not cleaned up in a short time, to avoid sickening the birds. Either feed very small quantities during wet weather or withhold it altogether, substituting other foods.

PEANUT HEARTS

Peanut hearts, the embryo of the peanut, are a by-product of making peanut butter. At one time they were a fairly standard feeder item, but their cost—about $.80 a pound now—has reduced their popularity. They're enjoyed by most birds that eat nutmeats. They have a tendency to spoil rapidly, but that's not really a major objection, since they also have a tendency to disappear fast. You may want to use them for an occasional treat, if not for daily fare. Some of the more expensive mixes labeled "high energy" contain peanut hearts. Such mixes are intended for use in severely cold weather. Safflower seed is sold at approximately the same price as peanut hearts. Although it too is a good food, its cost makes it little used.

SUET

"Bird" suet is widely available in northern supermarkets in the wintertime. Come warmer weather, it usually disappears, so you'll have to rely on an honest-to-goodness butcher shop, seed-suet cakes, or the suet you've providentially stashed in the freezer. Suet used to be free, like soup bones, but now it ranges from a quarter a pound up, depending on where and when you get it. We always have a considerable amount on hand because we raise our own beef. Be sure to demand suet (you've already paid for it, in the hanging weight!) if you buy beef by the side. If you buy seed-suet cakes, they'll range in price from $1.50 to $4, depending on weight. Some of them are self-contained, ready-to-hang units complete with perches.

COOKING FOR THE BIRDS

Before going on to some of the non-wild bird foods that can be fed to birds, let's consider some of the concoctions that people prepare in their kitchens especially for the feeders. In the last chapter I described the bacon grease, peanut butter, and/or cornmeal mix that's used in log feeders. Rendered suet mixed with cornmeal, peanut butter, or cracked corn can be poured into molds (tuna fish cans, margarine tubs, and the like) to harden. Feed it in suet holders or pour it before it hardens into such impromptu feeders as coconut shells. Commercial mixes of birdseed can also be used with rendered suet. Sometimes raisins, currants, and brown sugar are added. Try your own combinations.

Bird-cookery projects frequently appeal to children and other novice bird feeders. I suffered from the affliction briefly; but as chief cook for our family, I spend enough time in the kitchen preparing meals for the household, including dogs and cats. I can live without cooking for the birds as well. A minor compromise is possible, though. Birds can be fed certain table scraps and discarded items from the preparation of family food.

We have so many domestic animals that the garden birds don't often get kitchen waste from our household. If we didn't have dogs, cats, horses, cows, and chickens, however, the garden birds would get a lot of leftovers. I'm appalled by the amount of food that our friends and relatives pour down disposals or throw into their garbage cans. (Some of the items could at least go on the compost heap!) Others would serve at no cost, as part of a bird-feeding program.

The first item that comes to mind, because calcium is so important for birds, is eggshells. Toasted lightly in the oven, then broken up or crushed, they can be dispensed with other foods or included in those suet cakes you produce. It's believed that serving eggshells to jays will prevent them from robbing eggs from other birds' nests. During nesting time especially, it's a service to the birds to provide them eggshells.

Junior doesn't like bread crusts? The birds do. Crumble them and scatter them on the ground or in other feeding areas. Someone didn't finish his cake? The birds will be delighted. Almost any stale or leftover bakery product will find some eager consumer in your local bird population: doughnuts, muffins, biscuits, cornbread, pancakes, waffles, piecrust, bread, cookies, cakes—you name it. These are all made largely from grains, so it's not surprising that birds enjoy them. They should be broken or torn into bits so the birds can handle the pieces.

NEW FOODS

Birds tend to be suspicious of new foods, but if they're accustomed to eating in a particular place, they're likely to test an unfamiliar tidbit left there. Because kitchen scraps are likely to spoil quickly, especially in warm weather, put out only small quantities at any given time until you see what takers you have. Don't forget that some of these scraps, fed separately, may keep starlings, grackles, blackbirds, and house sparrows from monopolizing feeders. Try cooked potatoes in any form, sweet potatoes, cooked rice, meat scraps, pieces of fruit, leftover cooked or ready-to-eat cereal. Always be sure that scraps are in sizes appropriate to birds or else securely held in place so that they can be consumed a little at a time. Pieces that are too big will be dropped. Not only will that make your yard look trashy; it's bound to attract unwanted guests.

Among the kitchen waste items, don't forget seeds: apple seeds (you can serve them core and all), melon seeds, pumpkin and squash seeds. If the seeds are really large, putting them through a meat grinder will make them much easier for small birds to handle. If you dry them when you have excessive amounts, you can serve them later.

Speaking of waste seeds, we store hundreds of bales of hay in our barn for winter feeding of livestock. Over a few months, a great amount of chaff accumulates on the floor. It makes a welcome treat for the birds in early spring when natural food is scarce. I just sweep it out of the loft into the paddock. The ground feeders get to work on it quickly.

GRIT NEEDED

Remember that birds don't have teeth and they need grit to help them digest food. You can offer coarse sand in the feeder occasionally to help supply it, especially during times of snow cover. Crushed oyster shell is frequently recommended, but it's hard to find, even at many feed stores. Bits of old mortar are attractive to birds, and so are coal ashes. Both probably supply needed minerals.

Selective feeding will attract the birds you prefer. Many birds like nutmeats, and some that prefer insects will eat fruits and berries. These are expensive unless you can collect wild ones and hold them in the freezer or in dry storage for occasional treats. Grain foods attract the greatest variety of birds. Color is important to birds in selecting their food. You'll recall that white bread and white suet attract birds to brand new feeders. Many birds that like black thistle seeds are also attracted to rape and sunflower seeds, both of them black. Peanut butter and nutmeats seem to be the only brown foods birds really relish. If you put out a doughnut for them, for example, they're unlikely to sample it unless it's broken open so they can see the white part. (Many birds are partial to doughnuts once they taste them.) Brown breads appeal to them much less than white ones. Most birds prefer red fruit and berries to yellow, and hummingbirds go most readily to red flowers.

HUMMINGBIRD FOOD

Which brings us to the subject of filling your hummingbird feeder. Experts disagree on what to use—sugar or honey—and in what proportions to water. Some say there aren't any vitamins or minerals in sugar, but their opponents argue that honey can more easily ferment and cause various problems. The recommended ratio varies from three to nine parts water to one part sweetener. Commercial nectar, a concentrated high-energy sugar compound simulating flower nectar, runs $1.50 for eight ounces, $8 for 3½ pounds. An accompanying vitamin supplement formulated to counteract deficiences goes for $6. Whatever you use, make sure feeders are cleaned on a regular basis. And keep ants away; hummingbirds won't use a feeder that has attracted ants.

So there you have a brief description of various foods suitable for birds, their approximate costs, and some ways to serve them. If you're disappointed in the visitors you have, check the section on bird families to see who eats what and how it should be served. Then start selecting foods that will appeal only to the birds you prefer to feed or use methods of presenting food that discourage unwelcome guests.

WHO EATS WHAT

SUNFLOWER SEEDS
: Cardinal, goldfinch, purple finch, Harris's' sparrow, white-crowned sparrow, slate-colored junco, crossbill, cowbird, towhee, blackbird, grackle, mountain chickadee, black-capped chickadee, titmouse, myrtle warbler, white-breasted nuthatch, red-breasted nuthatch, brown-headed nuthatch, grosbeak, jay.

PEANUT BUTTER
: Cardinal, song sparrow, chipping sparrow, tree sparrow, field sparrow, dickcissel, mockingbird, black-capped chickadee, brown-capped chickadee, titmouse, myrtle warbler, pine warbler, wood thrush, summer tanager, Carolina wren, red-bellied woodpecker, bluebird.

NUT MEATS PEANUTS
: Goldfinch, purple finch, house finch, white-throated sparrow, slate-colored junco, bunting, towhee, red-winged blackbird, grackle, Baltimore oriole, catbird, thrasher, black-capped chickadee, Carolina chickadee, mountain chickadee, titmouse, myrtle warbler, orange-crowned warbler, pine warbler, white-breasted nuthatch, hermit thrush, Carolina wren, red-bellied woodpecker, red-breasted nuthatch, brown-headed nuthatch, starling, kinglet, bluebird, yellow-bellied sapsucker, red-headed woodpecker, mourning dove, blue jay, Steller's jay, mockingbird.

MILLET
: Purple finch, house finch, song sparrow, slate-colored junco, dickissel, cowbird, red-winged blackbird, field sparrow, goldfinch, fox sparrow.

BREAD, DOUGHNUTS
: Field sparrow, white-crowned sparrow, slate-colored junco, bunting, house finch, song sparrow, chipping sparrow, red-winged blackbird, mockingbird, thrasher, robin, wood thrush, red-bellied woodpecker, cardinal,

Carolina wren, tree sparrow, brown-capped chickadee, titmouse, myrtle warbler, orange-crowned warbler, white-breasted nuthatch, pine warbler, grackle, catbird, black-capped chickadee, brown-headed nuthatch, bluebird, summer tanager, red-headed woodpecker, purple finch, mockingbird, blue jay.

HEMP
Red-winged blackbird, tree sparrow, Harris's' sparrow, goldfinch, cowbird, house finch, purple finch, song sparrow.

FRUIT
House finch, towhee, red-winged blackbird, summer tanager, yellow-bellied sapsucker, Baltimore oriole, robin, Western tanager, catbird, mockingbird, starling, red-bellied woodpecker, red-headed woodpecker, dove, bluebird, fox sparrow, Steller's jay, hermit thrush.

THISTLE
Finch, sparrow, chickadee, titmouse, towhee, junco, mourning dove.

CRACKED CORN
Red-winged blackbird, grackle, thrasher, blue jay, red-bellied woodpecker, red-headed woodpecker, house finch, song sparrow, tree sparrow, fox sparrow, field sparrow, Harris's sparrow, white-crowned sparrow, white-throated sparrow, slate-colored junco, bunting, dickcissel, towhee.

SUET
Field sparrow, slate-colored junco, house finch, song sparrow, chipping sparrow, tree sparrow, grackle, mockingbird, catbird, California thrasher, black-capped chickadee, mountain chickadee, brown-capped chickadee, orange-crowned warbler, myrtle warbler, pine warbler, white-breasted nuthatch, red-breasted nuthatch, starling, kinglet, wood thrush, hermit thrush, summer tanager, Carolina wren, red-bellied woodpecker, red-headed woodpecker, yellow-bellied sapsucker, Baltimore oriole, blue jay, titmouse.

WHEAT
Slate-colored junco, dickcissel, Harris's sparrow, grackle.

OATS	Dickcissel, black-capped chickadee, chipping sparrow.
PUMPKIN SEEDS	Tree sparrow, purple finch, black-capped chickadee.
SQUASH SEEDS	Purple finch, black-capped chickadee, bluebird.
RAISINS	Wood thrush, catbird, thrasher, mockingbird, red-winged blackbird, robin.
CHEESE	Catbird, thrasher, Carolina wren.
SCRATCH FOOD	Purple finch, cardinal, cowbird.
WEED SEEDS	White-throated sparrow, fox sparrow, dove, field sparrow.
MIXED SEEDS	Bunting, towhee, starling, kinglet, California thrasher, black-capped chickadee, red-bellied woodpecker.
GRAINS	Rusty blackbird, mockingbird, California thrasher, red-headed woodpecker, dove.
CHERRY & AUTUMN ELAEAGNUS	Cardinal, bluebird, flicker, catbird.
DATE PALMS	Bluebird, robin, waxwing, mockingbird.
MOUNTAIN ASH	Bluebird, flicker, waxwing, Western tanager, hermit thrush.
BLACK GUM	Bluebird, robin, flicker, hermit thrush.
CAMPHOR TREES	Bluebird, robin.
CHINESE & SIBERIAN ELMS	Goldfinch, waxwing.
DOGWOOD & SUMAC	Hermit thrush, wood thrush.
VIRGINIA CREEPER	Hermit thrush, flicker, robin, bluebird.
BITTERSWEET	Hermit thrush, bluebird, robin.
COTONEASTER	Robin, bluebird, waxwing.
BIRCH & ALDER	Fox sparrow, goldfinch.

GROUND MEAT	Baltimore oriole, Carolina wren, starling.
DOG FOOD	Red-winged blackbird, California thrush.
CORNMEAL	Myrtle warbler, pine warbler, wood thrush.
SUMAC & *GOLDENROD* *SEEDS*	Myrtle warbler, wood warbler.
SPRUCE, PINE, *FIR, MAPLE SEEDS*	White-breasted nuthatch, red-breasted nuthatch.
BERRIES	Indigo bunting, white-throated sparrow, towhee, chipping sparrow, starling, kinglet, bluebird, flicker, Carolina wren, Baltimore oriole, California thrasher, mountain chickadee, cardinal, waxwing, wood thrush, mockingbird, black-capped chickadee, myrtle warbler, red-headed woodpecker, robin, blue jay.

4
The
Water Situation

Oddly enough, many people who want to attract birds neglect to provide water for them. They may have multiple feeders, which they conscientiously stock year in and year out; and yet they fail to furnish water, which is as important to the birds and sometimes harder to find than food. There are, in fact, birds that will ignore all your efforts to entice them to food delicacies but will readily visit a birdbath to drink and disport themselves with abandon.

To provide water is the least expensive method of attracting birds. Oh, you *can* go to a lot of trouble and expense, but it isn't really necessary. The amounts needed are small and, most of the time, serving is simplicity itself.

I confess that, for a long time, I was guilty of ignoring this simple, effective method of attracting birds. We live in a rural area laced with brooks and ponds. A wide trout brook runs through our land behind the back pasture. Most winters it freezes fairly early, despite the fact that it's fast and moderately wide, with deep pools here and there. The problem didn't strike me as particularly significant. There are, after all, stock tanks for the horses and cows, kept at 40° F. all winter by floating heaters. It took me a while to discover that garden birds don't like to drink from stock tanks. One of the reasons it came as a surprise is that our barnyard flocks of Rhode Island Reds, Buff Orpingtons, and Australorps fly up to the tanks for refreshment at least as often as they use their own facilities. I had also noticed, occasionally, a sparrow or other small bird drinking at the stock tanks. Every so often (quite infrequently), we found a dead bird, domestic or wild, in the water.

SHALLOW WATER

The fact is that most of the birds that come to feeding stations prefer to drink—and bathe—in very shallow water. If you've observed songbirds drinking at a brook or some other natural water source, you'll have noticed that most of them use the edges. The majority of garden birds prefer the water to be no more than 2½ inches deep. Even large birds like jays and grackles are highly suspicious of water more than four or five inches deep. All of them prefer a vessel that *slopes* to the deepest point. Moreover, its surface should be rough so that they can easily keep their footing.

These modest requirements are very easy to fulfill. A run-of-the-mill birdbath of buff-colored clay, a shallow bowl separate from its pedestal base, costs about $20. The bowls are also sold separately for about $11. There are two reasons for this: the tops can, under certain conditions, be used alone, on the ground; they are also breakable and somewhat more prone to damage than the bases. Decorated birdbaths of clay are slightly more expensive, starting around $23 (bowls, $13). Concrete birdbaths are competitive in price with clay ones. That's the bare beginning. Anyone interested can find baths ranging from the tasteful to the bizarre, made from a wide selection of materials, and priced accordingly.

The use of the pedestal-type birdbath is recommended wherever there are cats because birds with wet feathers fly poorly; besides, they frequently become so engrossed in their bathing activities that they aren't as alert as they might be. The bath itself should be in an open area, on a lawn for example, so the birds are less likely to be caught by surprise. In placing a birdbath, make sure that there are trees or sturdy bushes nearby where the birds can preen after bathing.

HANGING BATH

Duncraft makes a hanging bath, sixteen inches in diameter and 2½ inches deep, of translucent plastic. It's suspended from a four-foot chain, costs around $20, and doubles as a feeder. I've never seen one in use, but it's a handsome thing and an interesting idea.

Containers other than birdbaths can be used for water. The larger sizes (say, six–twelve inches in diameter) of earthenware saucers made for potted plants work fine. Even with only half an inch of water in them, birds will find them quite satisfactory. Robins, catbirds, orioles, and grosbeaks are among those that find such saucers adequate for bathing as well as drinking. Garden pools can be constructed simply and attractively to beautify the garden and satisfy the birds at the same time. Keep them shallow, and sloping. If there is dry space around the edges, so much the better. Birds are very cautious in entering water to bathe, even when they are regular visitors to the site.

CLEANING THE BATH

Plastic or metal containers can be used if you place bricks or stones in the bottom to provide a rough surface. Pebbles or coarse sand would work just as well, but either is a nuisance when it's time to clean the container. (A "Jonnyring" perch is available to fit standard birdbaths. Theoretically, it will help keep the water free of droppings.) How often the bath must be cleaned depends on what birds use it and where it's placed. Most people prefer to have them some little distance from a feeder so that they'll stay cleaner.

Birdbaths seem to get the most business when the feeder is busiest, which isn't surprising. You want a cup of coffee or a glass of milk with your lunch, too. Grackles sometimes dunk their food before eating it. If they consider a piece of bread too hard, they'll carry it to the birdbath. That kind of behavior can make a mess in short order, but it's not as bad as another of their habits. They often dispose of various bits of trash, including fecal sacs from their nests, in birdbaths. To their credit, they sometimes eat—or simply remove—objects they find in the water. Other dunkers include starlings, house sparrows, and red-winged blackbirds. It's usually baked goods that get the water treatment.

Among the birds likely to visit birdbaths are some of the particularly colorful ones and some that seldom visit feeders. Included are bobwhites, bulbuls (exotic immigrants to southern Florida), indigo buntings, spotted orioles, brown thrashers, and cedar waxwings. Meadowlarks are attracted to lawn sprinklers, and white-winged doves will come to surface water.

FOUNTAINS

Among the refinements often suggested for birdbaths are fountains. When I priced them, out of idle curiosity, at a garden store, I found that very simple but handsome ones ran from $100 to $175. That had a dampening effect on my enthusiasm, although in theory the idea appeals enormously to me.

In the meantime, however, I remind myself that the *sound* of water may attract more birds than would ordinarily come to the birdbath. I may be enamored of a fancy fountain, but the birds couldn't care less about its aesthetic attributes. And there's a virtually cost-free solution to the situation that's very easy to manage. A drip will serve. Water dripping into a birdbath at the rate of about a drop a second is considered irresistible to birds. There are various ways to arrange the attraction.

There's the garden hose, for one. It doesn't make an entirely satisfactory arrangement, but it does make it easy to clean and fill the bath. It looks a little peculiar—or careless—and you'll have to move it every time you mow the lawn. I've heard of people getting around this problem by complicated plumbing intricacies—burying hose or pipe and then running it up to the basin at the pedestal. Personally, I can't face the idea of extensive excavations just for a drip. For a proper fountain, okay, but not for a drip.

A CHEAP DRIP

There's another way to go about the drip project. It's not necessarily a perfect solution from every point of view, but try to keep an open mind. For one thing, the mechanism can be camouflaged. It *should* be. Here's how we did it. My husband, Bud, took a three-pound coffee can. Like most coffee cans, it was colorful—bright blue, with red accents. Such lurid colors are apt to alarm birds, and they don't do much to improve the premises, either. Bud sprayed it flat black. Dull green or brown would be okay too. He fashioned a wire bail for it and punched two holes near the top of the can in which he fastened the wire. Then he punched a tiny, a nearly infinitesimal, hole in the bottom of the can, slung the bail over the conveniently overhanging limb of a crab apple tree, and filled the container with water. What resulted was a steady stream, albeit small, instead of an alluring *plink, plink.*

An ingenious fellow and not one to be foiled by a mere coffee can, he took a sheet metal screw and a rubber washer and inserted the screw from the outside through the washer and the hole in the

coffee can. By a simple twist of the screw, the drip can be regulated. There's no need to take a screwdriver to it, either. Since the screw protrudes through the bottom of the can, grasping it and turning it will suffice. It's worth noting that the drip will require attention the first couple of days because the washer swells very gradually as it becomes sodden. As far as we know—we didn't mount a twenty-four-hour watch—it took the birds two days to discover their new recreation center. The first visitor we noticed was an adolescent robin. He enjoyed himself immensely, splashed vigorously, and then retreated to the crab apple tree to rearrange his feathers. The birds congregate in the area, part of our formal garden, and merely hop or fly short distances away when we're mowing, weeding, or simply visiting the place.

The drip is likely to attract birds that might otherwise ignore your birdbath. Warblers of various kinds, depending on season and area, flycatchers, and thrushes other than robins may be among the visitors. The sound of the water gets their attention, and its movement may also enhance its appeal.

STONE BASINS

Besides ordinary birdbaths, basins, saucers, and pools, some birders report that natural stone basins which hold only a small amount of water attract the birds. Such natural basins and shallow pools are easy to clean with a stiff broom. One warning: friends of ours came home from a weekend at their beach cottage to find a catbird drowned in their children's plastic wading pool. Apparently it had misjudged depth and was unable to get out.

What happens if you don't provide water? If the birds stick around your place despite this oversight, they're more likely to eat your small fruits and berries to get moisture. They'll "bathe" in wet foliage after a rain. Thirst is probably regulated by the birds' diet. Goldfinches, primarily seed eaters, need a lot of water. Birds such as bluebirds, that eat primarily fruit and insects, will not need as much water. In naturally dry areas, water may be *all* you need to attract birds. In other areas, however, the birdbath will get more of a workout at some times than at others. During times of sparse rainfall, for example, you can expect record attendance. During the fall months, water may attract more migrants than your feeding station does (because of the abundance of natural foods). Birds will use the water about three times as often for drinking as for bathing. In the summertime, they will bathe most often on cool days. Evidently they're not fond of warm water for the purpose and, of course, water warms up quickly in a shallow container. Birds seem to feel a need for bathing most at molting time, in August and September. Presumably it has a soothing effect on skin made sensitive by the molt.

HOW THEY BATHE

It's entertaining to watch the different approaches various birds have to bathing. Hummingbirds, as you might expect, prefer to perform the rite "on the wing." If you have a fountain, or use a lawn sprinkler, you may see them flying through it, just as they fly through the mist of waterfalls. Phoebes and kingbirds—seldom feeder visitors—like the same method.

Flycatchers fly down to the birdbath, smack the water soundly with their breasts, and then fly to a perch. They often repeat the performance. Wrens, titmice, and chickadees are in and out quickly. Cedar waxwings usually arrive in flocks, to feed or to bathe. They'll wait their turns at the birdbath, but once in it they're every bit as exuberant as catbirds. Cardinals prefer to bathe alone. Chipping, white-throated, and song sparrows can be described as compulsive bathers. The song sparrows are so fond of the activity that they try to drive other birds away. Starlings are so obstreperous in their bathing that the bath often must be replenished (and scrubbed!) after they finish their ablutions. You'll probably see house sparrows enjoying the shower that the starlings create by their splashing. Warblers, juncos, thrashers, and orioles will be conspicuous frequenters of the birdbath.

FRESH WATER

Keeping water fresh and abundant isn't much of a chore during warm weather. Those of us who endure cold winters have a problem in supplying the birds when the temperature drops below freezing. If there's snow cover, the birds will get along fine. Some of them—downy woodpeckers, crows, juncos, white-throated sparrows, and black-capped chickadees—will even bathe in snow. But when the ground is bare and natural water sources are frozen, the birds may be in desperate straits.

There are various solutions to the problem. One answer is to put out *hot* water during freezing weather. But the container will be a problem. Clay and concrete baths will break if we try to keep them operating in winter by such means. The shallow black pans made by Fortex are splendid for bird watering in freezing weather. They're made of virtually indestructible, heavy, rather soft neoprene-type plastic. A solid blow to the container will remove ice without damaging Fortex in the slightest. You may pour boiling water into it with aplomb.

The highly respected John K. Terres in *Songbirds in Your Garden* (New York: Thomas Y. Crowell, 1968) speaks of the birds standing in hot water in extremely cold weather, apparently warming their feet and enjoying the rising steam. I feel diffident about questioning such an authority, but that's a situation that would make me feel extremely nervous. With no evidence to support my conviction, I'm persuaded that such a footbath might actually damage the birds' feet, perhaps inviting frostbite. John V. Dennis in *Beyond the Bird Feeder* (New York: Alfred A. Knopf, 1981), for example, reports that starlings that bathed in a heated birdbath when the air temperature was –10° F. promptly froze to death. In the same book he states the startling observation that, in general, birds are very active bathers when the temperature registers from 23°–26° F. Dennis asserts that birds bathe regularly in winter to keep warm: proper care of their feathers helps to insulate them from the cold.

WATER HEATER

If you will be away from the house and unable to provide fresh water in freezing weather when there's no snow cover, you might want to consider using an immersion heater in your watering facility. They are available for around $23 at both stores that sell poultry supplies and those that sell wild bird supplies. Relatively inexpensive to operate, they maintain a fixed water temperature of 50°–55° F. They can be used in containers that don't normally make good birdbaths. A metal or plastic dishpan, six to eight inches deep, is fine. Put the heater in the bottom with a layer of bricks or stones covering it to provide the correct water depth— about 2½ inches—for songbirds. Friends of ours use a large pail instead and float a block of wood on the water. Most of their winter visitors perch on the rim of the pail to drink, but a few of the smaller birds use the wood block itself as a perch. We use floating thermostatically controlled heaters in our stock tanks in winter, but the tanks themselves have now been placed in the barn. If they were outdoors, I'd float lengths of plank in them to give the birds a perch and an island of safety.

If you decide to heat water for the birds electrically, make sure you use a UL-approved heater *designed* to be immersed in water. Make sure your extension cord is of the outdoor, weatherproof variety. Don't try to cut corners and concoct a Rube Goldberg heater which may be dangerous to you as well as to birds and animals.

DUST BATHS

Birds engage in various other kinds of "bathing." While it has nothing much to do with water, it does seem to be related to feather care. Probably everyone has observed domestic chickens luxuriating in dust baths. If the procedure doesn't actually rid them of lice and mites, apparently it relieves discomfort. Chickens and their relatives, all of which are considered game birds—grouse, partridges, pheasants—are addicted to dust bathing. Indeed, they are offended by the whole idea of bathing in water. House sparrows are the only birds common to our gardens that are similarly inclined. You may have come across the little depressions they make in bare earth.

Birds can sometimes be seen bathing in smoke or steam. A more commonly observed form of bathing among birds, referred to as air bathing, is apparently stimulated by the sight of water and/or the sight of other birds bathing in water. While stationed on a branch, the ground, or some other dry surface, the air bathing

bird goes through all the motions of bathing in water. He then proceeds to preen his feathers, just as if he had become thoroughly soaked.

One may also observe sunbathing in birds, especially in hot weather, oddly enough. The birds squat down—often on the ground or some other flat surface, such as a roof—and, drooping their wings, fluff out their feathers in an apparent effort to expose as much area as possible to heat and sunlight. Whole flocks (*small* flocks, to be sure) have been seen sprawled out as if dead on lawns, feathers awry. Occasionally they shift position in order to expose fresh portions of their anatomies. They don't look particularly comfortable, but how many sunbathers do?

All of these bathing behaviors are necessary to keep the birds' feathers in proper condition. Animals, we may assume, are motivated to keep their coats—of whatever material they may consist—in a proper condition to protect themselves. Horses roll to relieve itches resulting from hot hides, insect bites, or shedding. They'll resort to wet places for a nice layer of dirt to assist thin summer coats in warding off fly bites. Pigs protect their virtually hairless skins from too much sun with a covering of mud. Dogs and cats groom themselves relentlessly. Just so, birds groom their feathers both to keep them in top flight condition and to relieve discomfort. They preen after their baths, whether in water, air, or sun. Most birds have an oil gland above the base of their tails. They massage it with their beaks and then run their beaks through their feathers to waterproof them.

ANTING

One of the really peculiar behaviors associated with grooming is the procedure known as "anting." This is not to be observed commonly, but it's something that we can be on the lookout for. Most of what is known about anting has been reported by conscientious amateur birders, not by professional ornithologists. (We're useful to science as well as to the birds if we take them seriously and record our observations carefully.)

Both active and passive forms of anting have been recorded. In the passive variety, the bird plunks himself down in the midst of an anthill and permits—or invites—the insects to stroll through his plumage. In the active form of anting, the bird picks up an ant in his beak, passes it through his feathers, and then either discards it or eats it. Anting has been observed in blue jays, starlings, catbirds, robins, house sparrows, and juncos. Starlings take the prize for entertainment value in this category. Apparently convinced that there aren't enough ants to go around, they'll quarrel over a single individual. Once actually in possession of an ant, they are apt to become so engrossed in their activity, so eager to reach the unreachable itch, that they fall all over themselves. Starlings are little noted for grace or dignity.

Dedicated professional ornithologists, as well as amateurs, have often waited for years for the chance to observe birds in the process of anting. Apparently, the activity hasn't been observed in Florida, New England, or in the Pacific Coast region. Whether it doesn't occur in these areas or simply has not been observed and reported isn't known. Anting has most commonly been observed on anthills or in favored sunning sites, from mid-May through August, in periods of high humidity. Some observers have wondered if the activity were related to thunderstorms. It's supposed that it *is* related to skin irritation, but whether to the actual presence of skin and feather parasites or to molting hasn't been discovered. A combination of factors would seem to be more likely, considering the time period during which anting has been reported. Birds don't usually molt until August and September. Anting, by the way, is not confined to birds. This strange behavior has been observed in two bird enemies, gray squirrels and domestic cats.

Related, probably, to anting is the practice of using other materials to groom or soothe the skin. What seems to be common to the items used is a heat-producing quality. The birds are thought to stumble on appropriate material through the process of trial and error. Among the articles that have been recorded by observers are pieces of the rind of limes and other citrus fruits, sumac berries, chokecherries, apple peel, green English walnuts, and pieces of raw onion, to say nothing of moth balls, mustard, vinegar, pickles, and beer. Blue jays (wouldn't you know it would be blue jays!) have been photographed using still-burning cigarette butts. There's a heat-producing agent with a vengeance.

5
Learning
to be a Landlord

Food. Water. Shelter. Just as water attracts some birds to your yard, shelter will attract others. Providing nest boxes is particularly important for city and suburban folk who want birds around. Difficulty in finding natural shelter near the food and water sources you supply may tempt birds to look elsewhere for a more promising environment. If you can provide a place for birds to nest, you'll have the pleasure of seeing them frequently at close range and the advantage of allies in the war against insects.

For the most part, the birds that use nesting boxes are mighty eaters of insects. Under natural conditions, they'd be nesting in holes in trees or fence posts or telephone poles. You'll provide artificial holes for them. With just a little attention to detail, you'll be able to attract specific birds and exclude those you find less desirable. In the next chapter, we'll attend to natural foods and natural shelter in your yard. For now, we'll concentrate on what you build or buy and install.

The birds that accept birdhouses most readily are cavity nesting birds. Especially in city and suburban yards, natural cavities are hard to come by. Any trees old enough to have developed cavities of the right size are usually treasured by their owners. Tree surgeons will very likely have filled any cavities. Not much likelihood of ancient fence posts, either, and the utility companies replace poles regularly. That doesn't leave much for instant bird accommodations.

CHOOSING THE SITE

So it's up to you, if you want nesting birds. There's a little more to it than just hanging up a birdhouse. The site should be chosen carefully. Birdhouses hung in or fastened to trees should be clear of the main trunk, and should be where sunshine can reach them. One of the advantages of positioning new birdhouses in early autumn before the leaves fall is that you can make sure their locations won't be too dark and gloomy. All growing things need sunshine, including little birds. Entrance holes ought to face away from prevailing winds.

Life is more dangerous for nestlings and fledglings than for mature birds because they're less able either to recognize or to escape enemies. If only one or two of a brood survive to maturity, that's enough to maintain a species. We can help by offering protection against predators in the nesting facilities we supply. Make sure the house is safe from cats. If it's mounted on a post that cats or squirrels can climb, wrap the post with sheet metal or mount a cone-shaped metal guard beneath the house. The latter can be purchased from stores that handle bird supplies. Birdhouses hung in trees five feet or more above the ground are fairly safe from cats. Certainly they can climb the trees, but they have a dickens of a time jumping on or otherwise endangering birds while they're clinging to a branch.

SQUIRRELS GREATER THREAT

Squirrels are actually more destructive to nesting birds than cats are. Their acrobatic abilities are awesome, as anyone who has tried to keep them out of feeders will testify. Rats are another problem. They'll eat not only bird eggs and nestlings but sometimes, at night, the parent bird incubating the eggs. Rat control is one of many reasons to protect owls. The barn owl, which will dine on mice as well as young rats, is often considered the most useful of all our owls in this respect.

If birds ignore the houses you've installed for them, be patient. A brand new house may be viewed at first with deep suspicion. Once it's weathered a bit, the birds are more likely to accept it. For this reason, fall is an excellent time to erect new houses. Don't forget that nesting time varies not only with the bird species in question but with geographical location as well. For same-year occupancy, the houses ought to be in place no later than January in the southernmost tier of states, February in the middle tier, and March in northern states and Canada.

CATEGORIES OF SITES

Nesting sites are as variable as birds themselves, but they can be roughly grouped into four categories. First are those birds that use the ground, cliffs, or beaches. Among the ground nesters are game birds such as pheasants, quail, grouse, and turkeys. Some small birds such as juncos, sparrows, and warblers also nest on or very

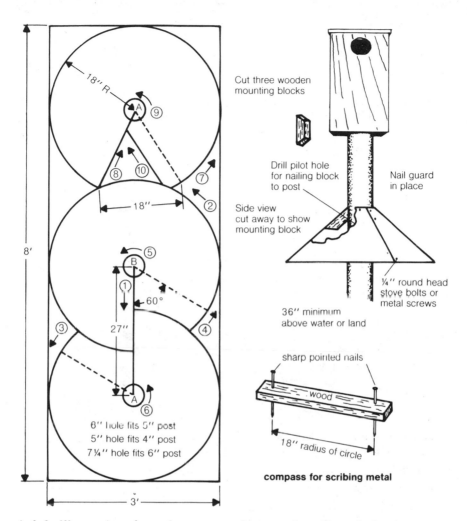

Cut three wooden
mounting blocks

Drill pilot hole
for nailing block
to post

Nail guard
in place

Side view
cut away to show
mounting block

¼″ round head
stove bolts or
metal screws

36″ minimum
above water or land

sharp pointed nails

wood

18″ radius of circle

compass for scribing metal

18″ R

18″

8′

60°

27″

6″ hole fits 5″ post
5″ hole fits 4″ post
7¼″ hole fits 6″ post

3′

At left, illustration shows how to cut three predator guards from a 3×8-foot sheet of 26-gauge galvanized metal. Scribe circles with homemade compass shown at lower right. Cut on solid lines, following the sequence of numbers on the drawing, and cutting the circles in a counterclockwise direction. To make first cut, on line A-B, make a slot at A with a cold chisel for inserting shears. Note, at left, the size of holes to cut for various sizes of poles. Above, at right, follow these steps when mounting the guard. First, cut three wooden mounting blocks, as shown, drill pilot holes for mounting the blocks to the post, then nail them to the post, at the same height and equidistant around the pole. Second, form cone around post, above the mounting blocks, and hold the cone's shape with ¼-inch round head stove bolts or metal screws. Third, nail cone to mounting blocks. (From Homes for Birds, U.S. Department of the Interior)

This simple predator guard (below) is a sheet-metal cylinder placed around the post holding the bird house. The cylinder should be at least 18" long and placed high enough on the pole so that cats can't spring over it.

This predator guard (above) is simply an extra piece of 1" wood placed around the entrance, making it more difficult for a big bird's beak or an animal's paw to reach the nest inside. Metal circlets can be placed around the entrance holes to prevent squirrels from enlarging the entrance hole. This can be dangerous to the birds if any sharp edges remain.

near the ground. So do the hermit thrush and some doves. We can't do very much to help them except to maintain such areas for them, safe from mowing and burning.

Another group, a large one, includes some favorite songbirds such as orioles, robins, cardinals, catbirds, mockingbirds, thrashers, kingbirds, hummingbirds, grosbeaks, and other finches. They prefer to nest in trees, shrubs, and vines and can be enticed to our yards if we provide adequate cover for them.

A third group likes an aquatic habitat such as a swamp. Not many of us can provide a swamp, but we can, in our towns, help protect wetlands for them. Apart from the herons, egrets, ducks, and gulls that you'd expect in such habitats, you'll also find the yellowthroat, blackbirds, some sparrows, and boat-tailed grackles.

Birds that will use birdhouses, the cavity nesting birds, are in the fourth category. These include many familiar garden birds: bluebirds, chickadees, nuthatches, wrens, tree swallows, titmice, flickers, woodpeckers, starlings, and martins. Among the not-so-common species that will use birdhouses are great crested fly-catchers, sparrow hawks, screech owls, and wood ducks. What you get depends on the dimensions and locations of what you provide. But more on that later.

Some birds will use nesting shelves that we provide. These birds, not cavity nesters, include phoebes, robins, and barn swallows. Our houses and other buildings on our property are themselves part of the birds' environment, and some birds, without any encouragement from us, will find a place they consider suitable on a building. Chimney swifts have become so accustomed to using chimneys as a nest site that they are no longer known to use anything else.

Most of us have had experiences with birds using what we consider inappropriate nesting sites. When we were building a house in the midst of a heavily wooded area, a phoebe insisted on building a nest in the floor joists. The workmen removed it daily. Then came a spell when heavy rains held up work for over a week. When work recommenced, there was the phoebe nest, with eggs in it. The activity and noise proved too much for the phoebe; she abandoned the nest.

The next year phoebes used the top of the shutter outside our son Tom's bedroom window. He was pleased to be able to see the daily progress of the brood. Another phoebe nested in the horse shelter, a third in the goat shed. We've never built a shelf for phoebes, but we're always up to our knees in them.

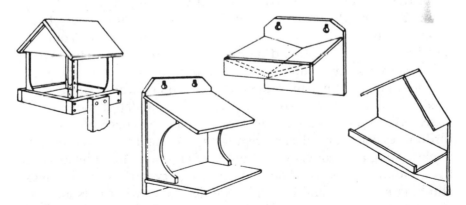

Phoebes, robins, and barn swallows prefer these shelves for nesting over the closer confines of a bird house. Two shelves on right are for hanging in areas protected from the elements.

Robins, too, frequently build their nests on houses or in garages. Friends in Amherst have a robin family in their carport every year. It's no particular problem in a carport, but a garage can be another matter, especially if you want to close the door. A couple of years ago, a robin in Illinois quite appropriately chose Mother's Day to begin her nest—in a hanging basket of flowers on a deck. She raised a family of three with no apparent difficulty resulting for birds or plants. I've known people who were unable to use a door of their house for weeks at a time because robins nested above it. If you don't care to suffer that inconvenience, remove the nest at once and hope the birds will find a better place.

PURPLE MARTIN HOUSES

The most conspicuous of all birdhouses are those designed for purple martins. The long tradition of providing homes for martins in this country started with the Indians, who hung up gourds around their villages for the birds. You could do that, of course, but there's something about a proper martin house that appeals to many people. For all I know, it may be partly snob appeal. These bird condominiums are so imposing that everyone can see you've gone to considerable effort to please the martins.

Before you rush to your workshop, ship off an order, or visit the nearest bird supply house, it would be prudent first to discover the probabilities of martins actually moving in. If you live in a heavily wooded area, forget it. Like other swallows, they like plenty of open spaces, and there should be water nearby. Your best bet is to inquire around the neighborhood to see if any martins occupy the large edifices you're bound to see.

If you find that martins like your area, you're all set. Start small, preferably with a house that can be expanded if the need arises. Martin houses are set on posts in an open space. Because all birdhouses should be cleaned regularly, you might find the use of a telescoping pole convenient. You can get a pole that adjusts from five to fourteen feet for about $30. Its slippery surface discourages climbing predators, and it comes complete with wing nuts and clamp to fit the brackets on the bottom of ready-built martin houses. The houses themselves usually have a minimum of eight

This eight-apartment mar-
tin house is made up of
four separate parts that
are linked together. The
parts are the roof, the two
stories, and the founda-
tion. Three-quarter-inch
lumber should be used for
the walls and floors, with
the roof and interior par-
titions made of half-inch
wood. The porches are 3
inches wide, with a half-
inch dowel serving as a railing and preventing the young martins from
falling to the ground. The central cross of the frame is made of double
thicknesses of ¾-inch oak, and the rest of the foundation made of ¾-
inch pine. The oak central cross is attached to the pole with four heavy
angle irons. This may sound overbuilt, but it is needed when the house,
weighing some 65 pounds, is placed atop a pole 10-20 feet in height. De-
tails of the house include a central air shaft and an airy "attic," to aid
in cooling the house, and a cove molding around the under side of the
roof and each story, to help hold the parts together. Hooks and screw
eyes fasten the units to each other.

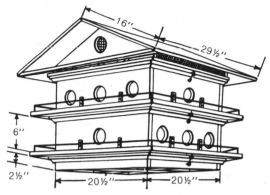

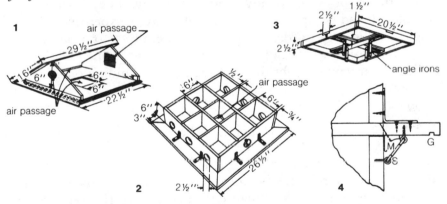

1. One side of roof is removed to show air shaft, slot under eaves, and
screened holes in the ends.
2. Chambers in each story are 6×6×6 inches, inside dimensions.
Note bottom of central compartment is cut out to form the air passage.
Entry holes are 2½ inches wide.
3. Sturdy foundation consists of an outer frame, an oaken cross, and
four heavy angle irons.
4. Porch can be attached to the house with angle irons. Note how molding (M) fits about the top of the lower story; the screw eyes and hooks
(S) fasten the units together. The groove (G) is made to prevent water
from draining inward.

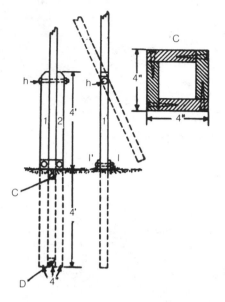
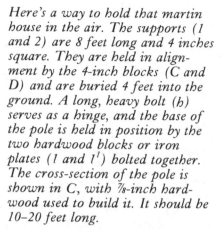

Here's a way to hold that martin house in the air. The supports (1 and 2) are 8 feet long and 4 inches square. They are held in alignment by the 4-inch blocks (C and D) and are buried 4 feet into the ground. A long, heavy bolt (h) serves as a hinge, and the base of the pole is held in position by the two hardwood blocks or iron plates (1 and 1^1) bolted together. The cross-section of the pole is shown in C, with ⅞-inch hardwood used to build it. It should be 10–20 feet long.

apartments and come in many different styles carefully calculated to suit the flavor of nearly any human dwelling. They start at around $50 and go up. And up. *All* real estate is expensive. Since single dwellings for birds, ready-made, generally start around $7.50, the cost of a martin house isn't really out of line. Those skilled in carpentry might like to have a go at building one.

BLUEBIRDS

Martin houses are the most conspicuous of all birdhouses, but the most common, surely, are bluebird houses. The reasons for their popularity are numerous. Bluebirds, whether eastern, western, or mountain, are very attractive creatures, inordinately pleasing to most of us, with a song evocative of spring. Add to this the fact that they have problems, and you're bound to see champions springing up. Human population growth, especially in the eastern United States, has destroyed a large amount of bluebird habitat. The arrival of immigrant house sparrows and starlings heavily increased the competition for nesting sites, since all three birds have similar requirements. The spread westward of starlings and house sparrows has had its effect on mountain and western bluebirds, but the eastern has been hardest hit so far. The final blow came in the terrible winter of 1957–1958. Migratory birds froze to death by the thousands in the South. Bluebirds, whose diet is mainly insects and berries, were especially vulnerable. It's estimated that a third to a half of the entire bluebird population died.

Things got worse. Six dreadful winters followed. In 1963 we had the lowest eastern bluebird population ever recorded. Bird lovers, especially the North American Bluebird Society, started an active campaign to rebuild the ravaged bluebird population. Major efforts were concentrated on providing nesting boxes specifically for bluebirds, boxes so designed that they would discourage other birds. Teams of volunteers all over the eastern United States have since been building "bluebird trails." Selecting appropriate surroundings and requesting the owner's permission, they place bluebird houses at least 100 yards apart (some authorities recommend 400 feet). That distance is important because bluebirds have strong territorial drives and will engage in spirited disputes with one another if houses are too close together.

THE BEST HOUSE

Spacing is but one of the considerations in attracting bluebirds to a house you provide. Let's examine the house itself. The North American Bluebird Society has listed the dimensions you should adhere to in order to attract bluebirds and discourage others. They're shown in the illustration. I've seen ready-made "bluebird" houses advertised for $7 that don't meet those requirements, so take care when you go shopping. The North American Bluebird Society will send you plans for 50¢ or houses from $4.50 and up, depending on materials. That's one of the best buys available in ready-made birdhouses.

You may well ask why all the fuss about these dimensions? When they nest in tree cavities and holes in old wooden fence posts, surely bluebirds cannot command accommodations so meticulously exact. But we're talking about a bird whose natural environment has been modified, whose competition has increased—and one whose numbers we're trying to increase. The dimensions are designed to suit the bluebird specifically while making the house undesirable for other species. That floor, for example, is adequate for bluebirds, but house sparrows find it cramped quarters because their broods are usually larger. The 1½-inch entrance hole is too small for starlings to use. Eliminating the perch works no hardship on the bluebird but prevents starlings and house sparrows from landing to harass them at home. Placing the house only three to five feet from the ground level also discourages house sparrows, which prefer higher nesting sites.

There are other birds considered more desirable than house sparrows and starlings that may also have designs on the bluebird houses. In all likelihood, you'll want to provide other houses for them while keeping the bluebird houses available for bluebirds.

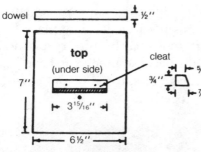

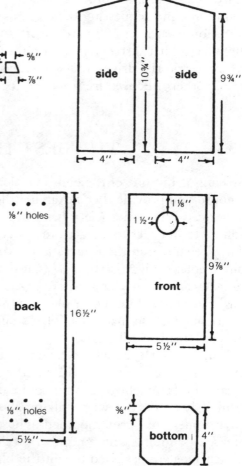

The careful carpenter can cut this birdhouse from a five-foot piece of board that is ¾ inches thick and 6½ inches wide. In marking for cutting, remember to allow for the kerf, the width of the cut made by your saw, usually about ⅛ of an inch. To build this house, you'll also need a ½-inch dowel 4 inches long, a cleat (cut it yourself) in the dimensions shown, a handful of 1¾" galvanized siding or aluminum nails, a 1½" wood screw with washer, and five 1¼" nails to hold the dowel and cleat in place. (From Homes for Birds, U.S. Department of the Interior)

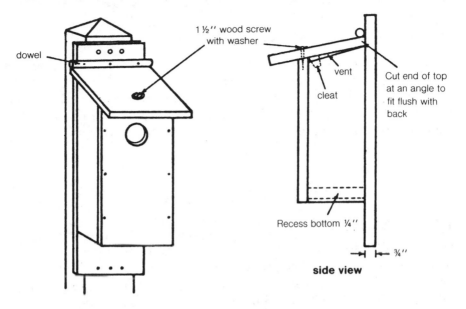

dowel

1 ½" wood screw with washer

vent

cleat

Cut end of top at an angle to fit flush with back

Recess bottom ¼"

¾"

side view

Construction steps
1. *Cut ⅜" off each corner of bottom.*
2. *Drill three ³/₃₂" holes in dowel for easy nailing.*
3. *Nail together back, two sides, and front. Note there will be an ⅛" gap between sides and top, in front, which provides an air vent.*
4. *Cut end of top at an angle to fit flush with back.*
5. *Hold top in place, position cleat for nailing by reaching through bottom of box.*
6. *Nail cleat in place.*
7. *Position bottom recessed ¼" and nail it in place.*
8. *Position top firmly against back and screw top to front.*
9. *Press dowel firmly in angle of back and top and nail into position.*
10. *Drawing shows ⅛" holes drilled in back for nailing onto post. Drill holes to fit your circumstances.*

To prevent wrens from claiming the bluebird box, avoid shrubby areas, which they like. Put it out in the open.

It's helpful if there's fence, tree, or shrub somewhere between 25 and 100 feet away from the bluebird box, in direct view of the entrance hole. The fledglings will have a place to land after that first flight. Have the houses in place early in the spring. Bluebirds are among the first to arrive in nesting areas and they get to work at once, often producing two to three broods. The houses should be cleaned out between broods. If you see evidence of lice or mites, dust the box with 1 percent rotenone powder.

BLUEBIRDS—OR SWALLOWS

Follow all the recommendations carefully and you just *may* get bluebirds. Then again, you may get tree swallows. (We do.) But they're nice, too. If you're a city dweller, however, you might as well forget about attracting bluebirds. They're far more likely to be found on farms, around old orchards, or in rural villages.

WREN HOUSING

Of all the cavity nesting birds that will use birdhouses, wrens are most likely to seek peculiar nesting locations. They've been known to use discarded shoes, tin cans, and the leg of a child's blue jeans hung up to dry. My Aunt Vi in Highland Park, Illinois, tells me that Uncle Sumner liked to use gourds for wrenhouses. He dispensed with perches but drilled "almost quarter-sized" holes, one to the front and one to the rear (not just one, the usual procedure). Hardly was the first one hung before a pair of wrens took up residence. Both birds worked together on hauling in nesting materials at first, but after a while the male took over the heavy work and the female remained inside, apparently arranging it to her satisfaction. According to Vi, it was quite a sight to watch him trying to maneuver a five-inch twig (that's easily as long as a wren!) into the entrance hole. Once he got it inside, his mate promptly chucked it out the other hole. They used both holes indiscriminately. Vi recommends hanging gourd homes from an old wire coat hanger snipped once just below the hook, on one shoulder line. This leaves one long piece of wire with the hook at one end. Straighten it out. Bend the snipped end to fasten to the gourd. Then you can hang it in a handy tree without needing to drag out the ladder.

A North Carolina wren couple built a nest in the middle of my brother and sister-in-law's brand new double pink vining geranium. Hardly had Bill placed the plant in a hanging basket attached to the overhang just above their front steps when wrens set up housekeeping. Mama laid her six pinkish brown spotted eggs smack in the middle of the geranium. Five of the eggs hatched. While the babies were still nestlings, Dee watered the plant very carefully, almost by droplets, in hopes of preserving it without damaging the birds. Four of the five nestlings survived to fledgling size and departed. When they left the nest, Dee investigated the geranium and found that the deep cup-like structure had displaced most of the soil in the middle of the plant. She replaced it and the plant, though scarcely robust, survived.

It should be clear that wrens are more easily attracted than purple martins or bluebirds; they are, in fact, more likely to take advantage of quarters you provide for them than any other bird. Usually, because of competition and territorial prerogatives, it's impossible to attract more than one nesting pair of any given species to a normal-sized lot. Not so with wrens. Some males will mate with more than one female and they don't seem to trouble themselves with separating the families to avoid scandal. With their cheerful song, amusing antics, and appetite for insects, wrens are welcome tenants.

Pairs of tree swallows, like wrens, will nest closer together than most other birds. It's best though, on a small lot, to supply them only one or at most two houses, 100 feet apart. If you're building or buying something specifically for these two species, as opposed to letting them do what they can with bluebird houses and geraniums, a house eight inches high with a five-inch by five-inch or four-inch by six-inch floor will accommodate either. The 1½-inch entrance hole should be six inches above the floor. Don't forget that all birdhouses need drainage holes and adequate ventilation.

WRENS AREN'T FUSSY

Every once in a while, even though wrens are far from fussy, someone reports difficulty in attracting them. Doris and Frank, in Illinois, hung a wren house. They heard wrens in their neighborhood, but for a couple of years their house remained vacant. One day Doris's sister remarked that they might have better luck if they turned the house so that the entrance hole faced south. They did that, and within *half an hour* a male alighted on a nearby branch and started singing, announcing his discovery to the world. He promptly brought nesting materials, which his mate just as promptly dumped out. It would be pleasant to relate that they raised a family there, but they didn't. Apparently they simply couldn't agree on the furnishings. It wasn't until two years later that a couple in agreement on such matters set up housekeeping and raised a brood. Don't give up too soon if tenants are slow to settle in.

Studies have indicated that wrens are partial to red and green houses and will use white ones only as a last resort. It's difficult to predict what birds will like in houses, but it's generally supposed that most prefer natural-looking ones. Chickadees, titmice, downy woodpeckers, and nuthatches apparently like a rustic-looking home, made of wood with the bark left on. Perhaps that's because they're woodland birds. They'll also accept weathered lumber, but no bright colors, please. The same dimensions acceptable to wrens and tree swallows will do nicely for chickadees, titmice, nut-hatches, downy woodpeckers, and prothonotary warblers.

NESTING BOXES

For larger birds, a nesting box fourteen inches high with a six-inch by six-inch floor and a two-inch entrance hole nine or ten inches above the floor will attract great crested flycatchers, star-lings, red-bellied woodpeckers, and hairy woodpeckers. On up the scale, a sixteen-inch-high nesting box with an eight-inch by eight-inch floor and a three-inch entrance hole fourteen inches above the floor will attract flickers, sparrow hawks, and screech owls. In-terestingly enough, both screech owls and sparrow hawks espe-cially like to occupy such nesting boxes in the suburbs or the city. Though their usual prey is insects and field mice, they *do* occa-sionally feed on small songbirds, so they may not be as welcome in urban areas as in rural ones. Though the diet of the two is the same, they're not competitors, since hawks work days and owls work nights. Rural dwellers who want to attract these birds should select a site ten to thirty feet above the ground. Orchards are especially good for the owls. The hawks like trees along the edge of a woodland or an open field.

You will find variations in size when you inspect plans for nest-ing boxes. The only area of real agreement seems to be on the size of the entrance hole required for each species of bird. The hole will exclude *larger* birds but not necessarily *smaller* ones. Make a big enough box and you can even attract wood ducks. The catch

NESTING BOXES

Species	Floor of Cavity (inches)	Depth of Cavity (inches)	Entrance above Floor (inches)	Diameter of Entrance (inches)	Height above Ground or Water (W) (feet)	Preferred Habitat Codes[3]
House Wren	4 x 4	6- 8	4- 6	1-1¼	4–10	2,7
Chickadee	4 x 4	9	7	1⅛	4–15	2
Bewick's Wren	4 x 4	6- 8	4- 6	1¼	5–10	2,7
Titmouse	4 x 4	9	7	1¼	5–15	2
Downy Woodpecker	4 x 4	9	7	1¼	5–15	2
Prothonotary Warbler	4 x 4	6	4	1⅜	4–12,3W	3,5
Nuthatch[1]	4 x 4	9	7	1⅜	5–15	2
Carolina Wren	4 x 4	6- 8	4- 6	*1½	5–10	2,7
Bluebird	4 x 4	8–12	6–10	*1½	3- 6	1
Tree Swallow	5 x 5	6- 8	4- 6	*1½	4–15	1
Violet-green Swallow	5 x 5	6- 8	4- 6	*1½	4–15	1
Ash-throated Flycatcher	6 x 6	8–10	6- 8	*1½	8–20	1,6
Hairy Woodpecker	6 x 6	12–15	9–12	1⅝	12–20	2
Great Crested Flycatcher	6 x 6	8–10	6- 8	1¾	8–20	1,2
Golden-fronted Woodpecker	6 x 6	12	9	2	10–20	2
Red-headed Woodpecker	6 x 6	12	9	2	10–20	2
Purple Martin	6 x 6	6	1	2¼	10–20	1
Saw-whet Owl	6 x 6	10–12	8–10	2½	12–20	2
Flicker	7 x 7	16–18	14–16	2½	6–30	1,2
Screech Owl	8 x 8	12–15	9–12	3	10–30	2
American Kestrel	8 x 8	12–15	9–12	3	10–30	1,4
Barn Owl	10 x 18	15–18	0- 4	6	12–18	4
Wood Duck	12 x 12	22	17	4	10–20,6W	3,5
Phoebe	6 x 6	6	(²)	(²)	8–12	7,8
Barn Swallow	6 x 6	6	(²)	(²)	8–12	7,8
Robin	6 x 8	8	(²)	(²)	6–15	7

*Precise measurement required; if diameter over 1½ inches, starlings may usurp cavity.

[1]Brown-headed and pygmy nuthatches (1⅛), red-breasted nuthatch (1¼), and white-breasted nuthatch (1⅜) will all use the same box. However, the smaller opening sizes where appropriate may discourage use by house sparrows.

[2]One or more sides open.

[3]Preferred habitat codes. The numbers in the last column refer to the habitat types listed here:
1. Open areas in the sun (not shaded permanently by trees), pastures, fields, or golf courses.
2. Woodland clearings or the edge of woods.
3. Above water, or if on land, the entrance should face water.
4. On trunks of large tree, or high in little-frequented parts of barns, silos, water towers or church steeples.
5. Moist forest bottomlands, flooded river valleys, swamps.
6. Semi-arid country, deserts, dry open woods and wood edge.
7. Backyards, near buildings.
8. Near water; under bridges, barns.

SOURCE: Reprinted from *Homes for Birds*, Conservation Bulletin 14, U.S. Department of the Interior.

is that it needs to be placed on a pole above water, conditions that few of us can supply. Your local Audubon Society will be glad to supply their recommended specifications on request. For ready-made houses, send for the free catalogue, c/o Service Department, National Audubon Society, 1130 Fifth Avenue, New York, NY 10028.

NESTING SHELVES

Shelves or platforms located in places safe from predators and reasonably sheltered from weather will be used for nesting by robins, phoebes, song sparrows, and barn and cliff swallows. Barn swallows nest in our horse barn every year. But there aren't as many barns as there once were, and many modern ones aren't left open, so the swallows have come to accept platforms as alternative nest sites.

Birds sometimes use houses or other buildings that happen to be on a property as nesting sites. Occasionally we have to take steps to prevent their using specific locations such as a light fixture or a door frame. But quite apart from nesting, birds depend on our buildings for shelter. In severe winter weather, areas around chimneys are particularly popular. Roofs, of course, are also used as perching and look-out sites.

The open barn is inviting to barn swallows.

WINTER SHELTER

Birds may use the birdhouses we erect for sleeping after they have raised their broods. Sometimes in inclement weather birds use the houses for shelter. Those of us who live in areas where winters are rough can provide roosting boxes to help small birds survive extremely cold weather. They should be protected from predators in the same way that birdhouses are. Put them in a sheltered location about eight to ten feet above the ground. Use an entrance hole three inches in diameter, facing south. The box itself should be ten inches by ten inches and three feet tall with the entrance hole placed two feet above the floor. Inside the box, install perches a quarter of an inch in diameter. Stagger them so that birds don't wind up on top of each other. Under some circumstances, such facilities can make the difference between life and death for songbirds.

NESTING MATERIALS

We can further help the birds in their nesting activities by providing them with nesting materials. Swallows, both barn and cliff, need mud. So do phoebes, robins, and wood thrushes. You can help them by placing a shallow pan in some accessible but out-of-the-way place and filling it with soil, preferably with some clay in it to make it good and sticky. Keep it wet. The birds will be appreciative, especially if a dry spell occurs at their nesting time.

A little pile of dry twigs will be welcomed by the wrens. Feathers are popular for lining nests. Swallows are particularly avid collectors. I've read that they prefer white feathers, but around here they make do with red and black and buff. Orioles, which usually use milkweed plants, will take string or twine, grass, cellophane, wood shavings, cotton yarn, and strips of cloth to weave into the construction of their elaborate nests. Robins, vireos, yellow warblers, chipping and song sparrows, goldfinches, and cedar waxwings also will use these materials. Some people drape the offerings over shrubs, but you can put them in a container nailed to a tree to keep things tidier. Make sure the materials are no longer than six or eight inches because longer pieces can form loops or nooses and strangle the birds you're trying to assist. Supply birds until August to take care of successive broods and late nesters. The birds may raid your garden for some odds and ends. They've been reported to use yarrow, rue, thyme, and pyrethrum in nest construction. Note that all of these plants are herbs that have insecticidal properties.

If all goes according to schedule, almost before you know it, there'll be babies in the nest. How long they stay there depends on the species. A number of birds—the marsh harrier comes to mind—lay and incubate eggs so they hatch at different times. This results in considerable variety in the nest. Most of our garden birds, though, hatch out all the young at one time. The nestlings mature quickly. Feathers can grow a quarter of an inch a day. In a mere twelve days, sparrows have fully developed primary flight feathers.

CARE OF NESTLINGS

Nestlings *do* fall out of the nest sometimes. What to do? If there's one thing few of us need, it's a baby bird to feed. It's a horrendous job, not always successful, but guaranteed to be full-time. Better to put the mite back in the nest. There's a widely held belief that the parent birds will refuse to care for young that have been handled by humans. This isn't so, according to the Audubon Society. Considering all the ramifications, it's far better to have the birds resume care of their offspring.

Fledglings need rescue more often than nestlings. When the young first try their wings, the future of birds seems in grave danger. What clods! A fledgling grackle attracted Tom's attention while he was mowing under the old sugar maples early in the summer. We brought the cats inside, but Tom felt that wasn't enough action. The young grackle seemed to have a strong death-wish. His parents were swooping around, scolding us, screaming encouragement to Junior. Junior seemed befuddled. We got a ladder from the barn and put Junior in the crotch of a maple. He didn't like it. He half-stumbled, half-flew to the lawn. Tom put him back in the maple. Indignant, he made it back to the lawn before Tom did. The adult grackles were, by this time, frantic. Since they had taken up stations in a tangle of lilacs, honeysuckle, and forsythia beside the driveway, we put the fledgling there. Eventually the parents calmed down. We saw no more of the youngster. They learn fast provided they survive those first dangerous hours, and will be ready to return in the spring to build their own nests and start the cycle again.

There we have it. Food, water, and shelter, all of it provided artificially. There are other natural approaches for those who want to attract birds to their property. If you're able to tackle at least some of the alternatives, you'll find them rewarding on many levels. Our next subject is landscaping with an eye to attracting birds. By looking to your garden for plantings useful to birds, you can achieve added beauty and privacy in addition to animated ornaments.

6
Gardening's for the Birds

You can have a garden full of birds year-round without placing so much as a single feeder. The trick is in planting trees, shrubs, vines, and herbaceous plants that will provide food for the birds. So why bother with feeders at all under those conditions? For the pleasure of seeing many birds of different species close up. You'll recall that it takes a lot of acreage to support any significant number of birds. To get variety and numbers requires careful planning and careful planting. The optimum arrangement is a blend of natural foods supplied by the garden and supplemented by feeding stations.

We've seen that water attracts some birds that normally don't come to feeding stations. Landscape features also attract certain birds rarely seen at feeders. They'll take advantage of natural food (including insects) or nesting and shelter sites. By attending to garden, water, and feeders, you can appeal to a tremendous array of birds.

As far as the birds are concerned, the very best gardens contain a combination of trees, shrubs, and lawn, as well as flower and vegetable plots. If you can add a brush pile or thicket and manage not to keep the surroundings absolutely immaculate, you'll have hordes of contented birds. (In theory, I approve of immaculate gardens. Since I seem incapable of ever quite achieving or maintaining that condition, it's comforting to realize that untidiness has its own rewards.) Songbirds live three to ten years and are perfectly willing to stay in an area that provides favorable food and nesting sites, or return to it annually if they're migrating species.

The coming of colonists to this country had a great effect on bird populations. Although settlers engaged in questionable practices such as introducing new species and hunting indiscriminately for food and plumage, they opened the continent to large-scale agriculture, which tended to provide more food for birds. Birds had had ample cover up to that time, but the largely uncultivated countryside hadn't produced enough food to support large bird populations.

Another change came with the growth of urban areas, still another with the widespread use of agricultural machinery. Cover disappeared not only with the cutting of forests but also with the disappearance of hedgerows between fields. When farmers and land owners got going with the wholesale use of herbicides and pesticides, the birds were in bad trouble.

75

It doesn't have to be that way, of course. We needn't stand by, assuming we're helpless against the forces affecting the environment. Not only *can* we do something, we *ought* to. Even from an entirely selfish point of view, we must realize that if the environment poses a threat to birds, it can't be good for us either. (Remember how the canaries used to monitor the atmosphere in coal mines?) You can figure that if your garden—or your city or town—has a varied and healthy wild bird population, it's a pretty

fair place for human beings to live. It's to the advantage of all of us, whether or not we can attract birds or maintain feeding stations, to join in efforts to protect natural habitat.

Some authorities on wild bird feeding tell us about the foods and techniques we can use to "wean" wild birds away from their natural foods and get them to visit our feeders for sustenance instead. I submit that such an approach is foolish, if not downright immoral. How much better it is to provide them with a choice, right in our own yards. Each of us can maintain a mini-sanctuary for wild birds. Growing plants that they prefer will give us the opportunity to enjoy more species at close range, without corrupting them. They'll repay the attention by the pleasure they give us and also by consuming insects, weed seeds, and even rodents.

We started gardening in earnest, on a half-acre plot, and got Peterson's *Field Guide* in the same year. The bird population seemed to grow in direct proportion to our advances in gardening. We counted on them as allies from the very beginning because we didn't like the idea of using pesticides. Admittedly, we failed to take into consideration the fact that the presence of birds doesn't guarantee an absence of bugs. Birds help to maintain a natural balance, but they don't discriminate between what we consider "useful" and "harmful" insects. At that point, neither did we.

It seemed like a natural progression, seeing birds in the yard, to add plants that would encourage them to stick around. But that's a rather different thing than saying we planned the yard for the birds. It was, from the beginning, designed primarily for people and their pets and domestic livestock. The birds happened. To assert their usefulness is actually beside the point. It pleased us to have them around, and most of us are delighted to find practical reasons for what pleases us.

The one time we started from scratch was fifteen years ago when we built a house in a clearing in the woods. We had trees, ferns, mountain laurel, blueberries, ledge, and a wet weather brook. At first we cleared only enough trees to put in house and driveway. Naturally enough, we saw only woodland birds—chickadees, nuthatches, woodpeckers. Gradually, over a period of several years, we opened up the area to make room for gardens and paddocks. As we got more sunshine and more open spaces, varied shrubs and herbaceous borders, the bird population became more varied. I was thrilled to see our first robin in that location.

OUR SANCTUARY

If we'd been actively hunting a place for a little bird sanctuary, we couldn't have done much better than our present home. It's a very small farm, with about six acres of lawns, gardens, and pasture, and the rest—another three or four acres—wooded. A splendid trout brook runs through the wooded area. What at one time had been a pond is now a marsh. To the west of us lies a large cornfield, to the north and east are the village and farms, to the south woodlands. Canada geese visit the cornfield in the fall after the harvest. Ducks visit the brook, and kingfishers and a few mallards make their summer home there.

Pheasants parade through the side yard, under the ancient apple tree. Grouse nest in the woods above the brook, red-winged blackbirds in the marsh. Mourning doves, phoebes, and kingbirds have their residences in the back pasture, swallows in the barnyard and front pasture. Occasional visitors include hawks and herons. Nearer the house, robins, grackles, starlings, orioles, and the other common feeder visitors make their homes. Because the character of the land is so varied, it attracts birds of open land, marsh, and woodland. In the years we've lived here, we've tried to make it more appealing to us and to the birds, but we can by no means take full credit. Both resident and transient species are determined at least partly by factors over which we have little control.

PLANNING PLANTINGS

An orderly process is best in planting to attract birds. In any landscaping efforts, it's sensible to start on paper rather than with a shovel, whether you're modifying an existing garden or beginning a brand new one. The same rules apply, regardless of where you start. Each of the starting places has its own built-in advantages and disadvantages. It's nice not to have to rectify past mistakes, your own or someone else's. On the other hand, it's pleasant to have the lawn in and some landscaping done. If there's a mistake, so what? You can live with it more easily than you can live with a void.

In planning plantings, take the house and any other fixed structures, such as driveways, terraces, tool sheds, and the like into consideration. Some plants that are most attractive to the birds are inappropriate near these features because they're messy. In all fairness, of course, the same objection can be made to certain plants that birds virtually ignore, such as the rose of Sharon. We have one that is a delight to the family but which has no apparent appeal to the birds. If that thing were near the entrance to the side porch, its falling blossoms would drive me frantic. Where it is, it does nothing but charm us. All the debris falls harmlessly to the ground. Good planning? Not on our part; some previous owner had the foresight to plant it where we could enjoy it without moaning over its faults.

Any property can serve as a sanctuary for birds. Sanctuary implies that the property supplies natural cover, adequate food (including supplemental food when it's necessary), and protection from natural enemies. The numbers and species of wild birds you attract will depend not only on the actual size of the property but also on the variety of its natural features. If you have upland green forage or aquatic plant forage, expect game birds in addition to songbirds. Flying insects will attract phoebes and, if there are wide open spaces, kingbirds and swallows. Terrestrial insects, including Japanese beetles and their larvae, are eaten by birds such as robins, cardinals, flickers, and starlings. Aquatic animals (if you have a brook) may well bring kingfishers; rodents and various other small mammals attract hawks and owls. Depending on your circumstances, the presence of songbirds themselves may attract some birds of prey.

Brush piles, weeds, tall grass, and dead limbs all supply cover to birds and to the things they feed on. Whether or not you're willing to supply such amenities will be determined at least partly by the amount of land at your disposal. What's no trouble on a large lot may be inappropriate (and look dreadful) in a small area. It is suggested, on general principles, that 8 to 12 percent of your permanent plantings should afford food or protective shelter for birds. Let's begin with the largest and most important of these permanent plantings—the trees. Some of them will provide food and nesting sites as well as shelter.

EVERGREENS

In colder climates especially, a variety of evergreens is useful, not only for bird shelter but also to add color and interest to your yard after the deciduous trees and shrubs are bare. Some gardeners choose evergreen shrubbery, but if you have the space, a selection of evergreen trees adds a welcome contrast in most climates. Pines, of whatever variety, are popular with practically all birds, and they also find favor with most people. Not only do their long

Pines are favorites of crossbills.

soft needles provide shelter from severe weather, but their cones provide food. Crossbills, possessed of uniquely shaped mandibles, are peculiarly well suited to feed among the conifers; but goldfinches, towhees, and chickadees are able to eat pine seeds also. Pines are favorite nesting sites for many garden birds, including grackles, jays, and tanagers.

The pine family includes, besides those trees identified by the word in their common names, several other familiar conifers. Among these is red cedar, a great favorite with a large number of songbirds considered desirable by most fanciers. Red cedar is a kind of juniper and, like juniper, produces berrylike cones. Spruces, firs, and hemlocks also belong to the large pine family. Balsam firs attract large numbers of birds—finches, nuthatches, game birds, grosbeaks, chickadees, and crossbills. Finches are quite partial to spruce trees. One northern conifer, again a pine, is a little confusing because it sheds its needles in the fall. This is the beautiful larch, or tamarack tree. Goldfinches find its cones irresistible.

SHADE TREES

A large number of favorite shade trees are as welcome to birds as to the homeowner anxious to beautify his property and make it more desirable. Generally speaking, the tall, handsome trees that have long lives take quite a while to reach maturity. Even while they are young and modest in size, however, they will prove worthwhile aesthetically and a boon to the birds. The oaks, synonymous with strength, boast over fifty species in the continental United States (some authorities suggest seventy-five species as being nearer the mark). Oaks are members of the beech family and are most common in the eastern section of the country. Mourning doves, flickers, woodpeckers, jays, titmice, nuthatches, and thrashers are among the birds that feed on their acorns. The American beech, a lovely native tree in the eastern United States, produces nuts eaten by game birds, crows and grackles, jays, woodpeckers, crossbills, grosbeaks, and finches. Best known, perhaps, next to oaks, are the maples, whose paired winged fruits are a favorite source of food to wild birds such as evening grosbeaks, purple finches, and pine siskins. Box elders, the maple family members common to the central states, provide food for evening grosbeaks. The flowers of the horse chestnut attract hummingbirds; the seeds of the white ash attract game birds, finches, grosbeaks, and cardinals. Seeds of American elms appeal to finches and cardinals. The Chinese and Siberian elms, which are resistant to Dutch elm disease, produce buds very much liked by goldfinches and Bohemian waxwings. Sweet gum, a handsome tree related to witch hazel, produces dry, round fruit full of winged seeds eaten by many songbirds.

SMALLER TREES

You don't have room for such enormous trees? Let's move down in size to the birch family. These wonderfully attractive trees produce catkins, green in summer, that enlarge and turn brown in the fall. Cardinals love them. So do crossbills, finches, grouse, nuthatches, and chickadees. All of these birds also feed on birch buds. The American hornbeam, also a member of the birch family, appeals to most of the same crowd. Hornbeams are relatively small, but alders are practically shrubs, except for those growing along the Pacific coast. They're all related and produce similar seeds and buds favored by the birds that like birches.

Black gum, also called tupelo or sour gum, is another medium-sized tree. Its fruit attracts bluebirds, catbirds, kingbirds, flickers, mockingbirds, robins, thrashers, and tanagers. With a track record like that, it's no wonder that the tree is popular with bird lovers in the eastern third of the country (excluding New England) where it thrives. Cottonwoods, of the willow family, are favored by ruffed grouse and evening grosbeaks.

Let's suppose you'd like some fruit trees. Peaches, apples, and pears attract birds, but plant a cherry tree—*any* kind of cherry tree—and word will travel to every bird for miles around. If you're counting on cherries for your own use, better protect some of the branches with netting. You'll get bluebirds, grosbeaks, robins, crows, thrushes, game birds, waxwings, and woodpeckers. The tree that's reputed to help protect early fruits and berries is the mulberry, a fast-growing tree whose fruit is as appealing to birds as anything you can plant. But don't plant it too close to your house or other fixed features like a patio; it *is* messy when the fruits drop. If you have the right kind of climate, you might want to grow date palms for bluebirds, mockingbirds, robins, and waxwings. Bananas will attract jays, mockingbirds, and orioles.

Nut trees generally take a considerable amount of time to produce a crop, but are valuable assets. Most birds like pecans and walnuts. Once the trees mature, there'll be enough for you too, provided you beat the squirrels to the harvest. Chickadees, finches, sparrows, nuthatches, wrens, woodpeckers, titmice, and some warblers like butternuts and cashews. Almonds will grow anywhere that peaches will, and the trees remain modest in size.

Cherries will attract the grosbeaks.

They attract cardinals, titmice, chickadees, crossbills, wrens, and warblers. Filberts, or hazelnuts, will command attention from jays, woodpeckers, and game birds.

ORNAMENTALS

Whether your garden is large or small, you'll surely want to find a spot to tuck in one or more of the smaller ornamental trees. They'll please you just as they do the birds. Try catalpa, a small tree of the trumpet creeper family, if it will grow in your climate. Evening grosbeaks think it's wonderful. In subtropical climates, the camphor tree attracts bluebirds, cardinals, robins, waxwings, starlings, and mockingbirds. Hummingbirds come to the chinaberry. Dogwoods are popular with songbirds, and so are magnolias in their various sizes and varieties. Hawthorns, actually members of the rose family, are an extremely varied group of somewhere between 165 and 1,200 species, depending on which authority you consult. You're almost sure to find one you can grow. Their fruits look like tiny apples and are eaten by many favorite birds. Locusts appeal to hummingbirds, titmice, chickadees, and game birds. Orioles, evening grosbeaks, and bluebirds are among the birds that feed on mountain ash. Redbud attracts game birds, cuckoos, and grosbeaks. Especially in combination with dogwoods, they're breathtakingly beautiful trees. Don't forget crab apples, which are lovely in the spring. If the waxwings discover a variety they like, they'll strip it of its fruit in a couple of days. Hopa crab apples are especially popular with them. Robins are likely to descend on Russian olives in the fall. If you have space for a little "wild" area, let the weedy sumac move in. Fifty species of wild birds feed on it. That's reason enough to keep it around, even if you didn't get the added bonus of brilliant color in early fall.

I suppose my bias is plain. Feeders that we place for birds are very important in any program to attract them to our environs, but the garden itself provides natural food and shelter while satisfying our own aesthetic senses. That's hard to beat.

You may notice that, especially in early spring when natural food is somewhat scarce, birds will eat the buds—both flower and leaf—of early bloomers like maples and fruit trees. It has been suggested that these are especially nutritious, but it's worth speculating that maybe the practice has more to do with availability than with nutritional value. It's not usually harmful to the trees. However, a correspondent of mine who lives in the San Fernando Valley in California tells about a large flock of robins that discovered his apple tree in full bloom and stripped it clean. It was one of only two times he had ever observed robins in his neighborhood. He suspects that they were lost at the time of their visit.

Before leaving the subject of trees, we ought to note that woodpeckers and creepers are among those birds that search out insects in *any* tree. Sapsuckers and woodpeckers make holes in trees, but many other birds (and squirrels) will use the holes to take sap or the insects trapped by the sticky substance.

SHRUBS

If you're not worn out from planting all those trees, you might as well dig some holes for shrubs in the empty spaces. Many of the fruiting shrubs appeal about equally to birds and people, a situation that may cause some consternation unless you net them for your own use or grow enough to share. We have two areas where raspberries and blackberries grow. The one adjoining the vegetable garden is largely ignored by the birds. I think the only reason they let that plot alone is that there are so many other berries growing wild behind the back pasture and around the edges of the marsh. They're undisturbed eating there, but the garden is often a site of human activity.

Our family is less than enthusiastic about gooseberries. We don't cover them and seldom see a ripe berry. The blueberries are something else again; we race the birds for the cultivated varieties. Bluebirds, robins, thrashers, and waxwings are attracted to the red currants, but we usually get enough for jelly. We grow two varieties of currants, one of which ripens much later than the other. If the first crop is adequate for our needs, we leave the second for the birds.

We also grow two varieties of bush cherries. One is primarily ornamental, and we leave the harvest for the birds. The other makes an excellent jelly. Both are attractive enough to earn a place in a garden strictly on their appearance; the produce is an added attraction which we welcome but don't always use. When we neglect to pick the cherries, the birds promptly take over the chore.

Various birds like elderberries. The cultivated varieties produce fruit more prolifically than the wild ones, making them a good choice for some gardeners. In our area there are so many wild ones that actually planting the bushes is superfluous. There seems to be plenty of fruit for man and bird. Cranberries appeal to robins, crows, sparrows, and game birds. The highbush cranberry attracts game birds and waxwings. Figs usually attract a great variety of songbirds.

Some of these fruiting shrubs, especially the prickly ones, provide excellent shelter and nesting sites as well as food. From the human point of view, they're useful and not much trouble to grow. A little pruning here and there is in order, but insect and disease problems are minor.

EVERGREEN SHRUBS

None of us can grow all of the things we might like to grow, and it may well be that you prefer shrubs that are more decorative than utilitarian. Many of us like to plant at least a few broad-leaved or needle evergreen shrubs, especially as foundation plantings. We've seen how valuable the needle evergreens are for shelter to wintering birds. Junipers also produce berries which waxwings and robins eat. You probably wouldn't have to be persuaded to plant azaleas in any case, but isn't it a nice bonus that hummingbirds like the nectar of their flowers?

Cotoneaster is another of the widely grown ornamental shrubs whose fruit is enjoyed by bluebirds, robins, waxwings, finches, and mockingbirds. Catbirds and cardinals

join the bluebirds in enthusiasm for both autumn and cherry elaeagnus. Euonymus in its multitudinous forms will also please bluebirds, as well as warblers, sparrows, and mockingbirds. Natalplum's outdoor range is restricted, but in southern Florida the bulbuls flock to it. Hollies have decorative fruit that many favorite birds find edible, but don't forget you need both male and female plants to produce fruit, borne only by the female holly. There are about fifteen varieties available.

Don't ignore honeysuckle because it's "common." No shrub is easier to grow. There are many different kinds of honeysuckle. You can whack it off to suit the space available, and you'll probably have to do just that; but you can let it grow however it wants to in that wild corner you've reserved. We have enormous clumps of it, bird planted, out on the brink of our marshy area. We also have it planted by the driveway. I'd hate to be without it, considering the way birds flock to it. Common or no, the robins, catbirds, and waxwings don't care.

Both Japanese and European barberry provide bird food, and so do cabbage palmetto, nandina, pyracantha, privet, rosa multiflora, serviceberry, viburnum, spicebush, and bayberry. Do be careful of the rosa multiflora as an ornamental, though. It's out to take over the world, and pruning it is difficult because the thorns are vicious.

As you can see, it may be more of a challenge to plant shrubs that don't provide bird food than to plant those that do. The choice is certainly large. I wouldn't dream of limiting myself only to those things the birds enjoy, but it's easy enough to include some of them and still have room for rhododendrons and mountain laurel, lilacs, flowering almond, and the like. At the very least, all shrubs produce perching sites for the birds. Some of those that don't produce fruit or seeds that songbirds eat (Japanese quince and rose of Sharon come to mind) attract hummingbirds to their flowers.

VINES

There are many more plants that bring birds to the yard. Consider the vines, such as English ivy, bittersweet, and trumpet vine. When weather permits, we like to eat our meals on the side porch. The trumpet vine that climbs up at one corner starts to bloom in July. For four to six weeks it blossoms with abandon, and the hummingbirds visit it often, not the least dismayed that we're dining too, not six feet away. If you want something better behaved, less flamboyant, try Boston ivy or grapes. There we go with competition again. We have no intention of going to the trouble of erecting a support for grape vines, cultivating them, and coddling them, without some personal return as jelly and snacks. Let the birds have the wild grapes, and protect the cultivated ones the best you can. If there are enough wild ones available and your domestic ones are close to the house, you won't have much trouble. By the way, the poison ivy vine produces a berry edible to birds. (That's one reason it's hard to control sometimes. It's often bird-sown.)

Many herbaceous garden flowers supply nectar to hummingbirds: bee balm, petunias, day lilies, dahlias, columbines, impatiens, and geraniums, to name just a few. Goldfinches delight in the seeds of cornflowers, cosmos, and coreopsis. Cardinals like four o'clock seeds.

ALPINE STRAWBERRY

One of the most effective edging plants I've grown is the Alpine strawberry. It provides delicious berries for the table and for the birds and at the same time is handsome and well-behaved. You can start the plants from seed in spring and be eating their berries by late summer. Alpine strawberry plants are everbearing. The fruit is small but has the fragrance and the sweetness characteristic of wild strawberries. Since it develops little flavor until it's dead-ripe, you'll probably have to race the birds for it. (There are yellow varieties that birds don't like as much, but we're interested in what they do like.) The plants blossom and set fruit all summer. Unlike most strawberries, the Alpines don't produce runners, so it's easy to keep them within bounds. Baron Solemacher is one variety; many seed catalogs list it.

VEGETABLES

Moving to the vegetable garden, you'll discover that the blackbirds are willing to eat your peas if they discover them. Goldfinches like catnip seeds. I've chased robins away from the first ripening tomatoes. (Birds all seem quite attracted to *red* fruit.) Mockingbirds, waxwings, bluebirds, and pheasants love asparagus seeds. It's possible, in my garden at least, to see a variety of birds feasting on dandelion seeds: buntings, goldfinches, sparrows, and nuthatches. Dandelions farther afield are likely to attract game birds.

Corn this high is bird-proof.

Depending on how much room you have, you may want to devote a portion of your vegetable garden to bird food. Practically all birds like corn, whether sweet or field corn. Some of them, unfortunately for us, like sprouted corn. Gardeners may have to protect the emerging plants until their root systems have developed enough to anchor them firmly. That gives you a chance to make an imaginative scarecrow. Aim for imaginative, since it's unlikely to be effective.

Millet is a grass-type crop which is very valuable as a bird food. You'll remember that its seeds are the base of many commercially available bird food mixtures and that there are many varieties. You can grow your own sunflowers and let the birds enjoy the

seeds after you've had the pleasure of seeing the flowers. Rape, oats, and wheat are other possibilities. For most of us, however, these are not much more than amusing projects to be tried on a small scale. It takes a lot of land and work to grow enough of any of them to be significant in a feeding program.

In reading about plants that birds enjoy in climates kinder than the one in which I garden, I've come across the blue gum eucalyptus, which is native to Australia but will grow (and quickly too) in warm, moist parts of the United States. It belongs to the myrtle family and its blossoms are filled with nectar. Waxwings eat the flowers avidly.

In the same book, the author casually mentioned tree tobacco and commented on how extremely popular it was with the birds. Now, one of the annual garden flowers I like very much is nicotiana, or flowering tobacco. I grow it because its fragrance is one of the most heavenly in the garden. I assumed that tree tobacco was a relative, maybe a relative *I* could grow, even in this climate, with a little extra care.

And so I could, theoretically—but not legally. It turns out that tree tobacco, beloved of the birds, is also called hemp. And marijuana. (See what a little research can do? Its value is incalculable—even though my family became *very* merry at my expense!) It is indeed a relative of my flowering tobacco. Botanically known as *nicotiana glauca*, it has become naturalized in parts of the southwestern United States, although it is not native there. As we all know, however, it's widely grown all over North America— yes, even in New England—and reportedly ranks fourth in the nation as a cash crop. However much it appeals to birds, it can hardly be recommended. You *can* buy hemp seed legally for bird food if it's been treated so that it won't germinate.

Some common ground covers provide food for birds. Clover in your lawn or a pasture is likely to attract game birds, as will vetch used as a ground cover. Starlings, grackles, and robins will search for insects in any lawn, and most of those they find are ones we'd as soon be rid of. An expanse of lawn not only sets off gardens nicely but provides a measure of safety for the birds because predators can't hide on it easily.

BRUSH PILE

That leaves only the brush pile. If you have a small yard, you'll probably want to dispense with that idea for aesthetic reasons, except possibly as a sometime thing. Larger properties can devote some out-of-the-way corner to a brush pile. It will provide welcome shelter, especially in winter. Some compromise is possible. If you have an area set aside as a vegetable garden, you might construct a small brush pile for the use of birds during the harsh months. A few branches, debris from the garden, and the discarded Christmas tree will be welcome as shelter for winter feeder guests.

It's highly likely that much of the landscape material you select because you find it attractive will be appealing to some of the birds you want to come to your feeders. You don't necessarily have to go out of your way to provide an environment suitable for the birds. If you find yourself in a position of adding plants to your garden, it's easy to select some that appeal to birds you especially like. In small gardens, it's sometimes a matter of replacing uninteresting plants or those with limited appeal with more desirable ones. The rule is, the more varied the flora, the more varied the visitors. How much time and attention you devote to gardening to attract birds will depend on your interest in gardening per se. If you have a plot of ground at all, something has to be done with it. Anything from a low-maintenance area to the most labor-intensive garden can be attractive to feeder birds.

7
Getting to Know Your Birds

An interest in birds is insidious, creeping up and catching you unaware. What I remember about birds from growing up in western Pennsylvania is cardinals and robins, pheasants and sparrows. Mother was forever telling me to come to the window to see the tufted titmouse feeding or bidding me look in the spiraea to discover the catbird. I was aware that she thought highly of both, but if the bird wasn't brightly colored, or ubiquitous like the house sparrows, I didn't remember it from one minute to the next.

In the urban areas where Bud and I lived when we were first married there were plenty of pigeons. At that time, for no good reason, pigeons vaguely annoyed me. They've had a bad press. So have the starlings, though I didn't yet recognize *them*.

MEET THE BLUE JAYS

In Michigan we lived on a quiet street. Our large backyard boasted towering pines. On one side we were adjacent to several vacant lots, on the other to an admirable garden. There were plenty of birds, but the only ones we recognized (no previous experience is necessary) were the blue jays. They'd been absent from our former homes and we thought they were grand, big and handsome and raucous. Later, in Virginia, we added mockingbirds to our list of interesting birds. We'd sit on the back steps and watch them for long periods performing their acrobatics above the telephone poles. They awakened us long before dawn with their songs. They also imitated, with dreadful accuracy, the most irritating sound in the immediate vicinity—the grating squeak of the toddler's tricycle next door. In all the places we lived, there were probably hordes of birds, maybe even lots of different species. I never noticed.

Then we moved to western Massachusetts and began to garden on a half-acre lot in a semi-rural area. There seemed to be an inordinate amount of bird activity. Grackles screamed from the white pines. Chickadees flittered through the dogwood branches. Downy woodpeckers drummed on the elms. A flock of evening grosbeaks descended on the apple tree one winter morning, looking like exotic tropical birds against the background of snow and dazzling sky and bare branches. It was a veritable revelation; I was hooked.

91

I went out and bought a copy of Peterson's *Field Guide*. Enough of this "yellow birds with black wings and white patches and beaks like parrots."

TIME TO LEARN

Maybe you've reached that same stage. You've provided food and water, and the birds have discovered your efforts.

You don't have any trouble recognizing the robin flitting around the birdbath. Or the blue jay busily—or greedily, depending on your point of view—carrying away sunflower seeds. But what about that little brownish bird? Sparrow, you think? But aren't there roughly ninety-three different *kinds* of sparrows? Or maybe it isn't a sparrow at all. Maybe it's one of those *other* little brownish birds.

Patrick F. McManus, in *A Fine and Pleasant Misery* (New York: Holt, Rinehart and Winston, 1978), talks about his mentor's novel system of ornithological classification. Certain game birds and birds of prey were normally identified by their common names, but the more exotic birds of field and forest got a different treatment. They were first broadly grouped as big, little, and medium-sized. When asked about a particular bird, the sage might reply, " 'Thet thar is what ya calls yer little black-and-white bird with a red head.' " McManus confesses his wonder that the man could always, and with obvious authority, identify any bird in question.

GET HELP

That's the state of the art with many of us. So what's the first step? An experienced birder is surely the best of all possible aids in learning to identify birds. But even if experienced guidance is available to you, there will certainly be times when you must have recourse to other methods. You'll want to know how to go about the process all by yourself.

In our household, books accumulate as readily as dust. What we consider the indispensible volume for identifying birds is Roger Tory Peterson's *A Field Guide to the Birds* (Boston: Houghton

Mifflin Company, 1947), now available in a new, expanded edition. If you don't live east of the Rocky Mountains, you would want its companion volume, *A Field Guide to Western Birds.*

The first thing to do is to familiarize yourself with the book. After all, there's no entry in the index under "small, undistinguished-looking brown bird." Browse awhile. There are brownish birds in Plates 45 and 46, but not *small* brownish ones. Aha! Plate 47 has small brown birds, and 57 and 58 are full of sparrows. You'll notice that the individual pictures of birds have black lines pointing to those conspicuous characteristics differentiating one bird from another.

Now, obviously, you don't intend to memorize every plate in the book. And if you go rushing for your field guide when you see an unfamiliar bird, chances are he'll be long gone by the time you find either the guide or the page in it that you want. So *look at the bird*, while you have the chance. Does it show any splotches of color? What kind of a beak does it have? What kind of a tail? Any discernible pattern? Markings around the eye, or head, or back, or breast? Stripes? Rings? Crown patches? When it flies, do you notice any particular characteristic, like gliding or dipping or

Check identifying marks on heads.

undulation? *Where* did you see it? Did any flashes of white or some color appear on wings or tail when he moved? What about his shape? Chunky? Slender? Did he walk? Hop? Perch quietly, or flit about? Did he say anything? What about size? Give yourself some mental image to compare the bird to. Was it about the size of a sparrow (5 to 7½ inches)? A robin (8½ to 10½ inches)? A crow (17 to 21 inches)? Make mental notes of all the physical characteristics you can notice during the time you're observing the bird and *then* consult your guide. See if you can find a picture. Then turn to the description.

That little brown bird was chubby. It had a slender beak. Its tail was cocked over its back. It *had* to be a wren. Song variable, like a song sparrow, but thinner . . . *thinner?* (You may find the written descriptions of songs helpful. They mean nothing to me until after the fact of having heard and identified the song. In either case, a recording of bird songs may prove invaluable. Your local library may have one, or be able to get you one. Cornell University Press has issued excellent records. So has Dover Publications.)

Let's see. Wrens are smaller than sparrows. But what *kind* of a wren was it? Did it have a white stripe over the eye? White spots in the corners of his tail? *Where*, pray tell, are the corners of his tail? Back to the illustration. Lo and behold, the handy black line shows you the corners of his tail. You were lucky to notice the angle of the little thing's tail, never mind white spots.

BINOCULARS NEEDED

What you need, of course, is field glasses, or better still, binoculars. Actually, binoculars are easier to find, unless you happen to stumble across field glasses at a tag sale or flea market. In any case, you need something to give you a clearer picture of the bird you're trying so hard to identify.

Binoculars come in several degrees of magnification, the usual being six, seven, or eight. You can get ten or twenty power, but they're more expensive and somewhat harder to use. Binoculars differ from field glasses (or opera glasses or a telescope) in that prisms have been added to the magnifying lens or series of lenses.

You'll be able to use them to advantage both earlier and later in the day, and what you're hunting will be easier to find because their field of vision is wider than that of a magnifying lens.

What does that mean? Focus your binoculars on the top of a telephone pole, say, a hundred yards away. Should you try the same thing with field glasses or a telescope, you'll notice that you can see farther to each side of the pole with the binoculars than you can with field glasses or the scope. That's important when what you're trying to locate has a tendency to move around a lot,

and is not apt to oblige you by perching right next to something you can sight in on easily.

You'll find a bewildering variety of binoculars available, in a wide price range. *Audubon* magazine (November, 1981) published an excellent article on the subject by Charles A. Bergman. Titled "The Glass of Fashion," it includes an exemplary section on criteria for evaluating binoculars.

That's not to say that field glasses and telescopes which you might happen to have around the house can't be handy gadgets. The other day we were trying to identify an uncooperative bird on a branch and our 8x40 binoculars simply didn't pick up the necessary detail at the range. Bud's spotting scope, at thirty power, did the trick. Especially in your own garden on a bright day, you can become quite adept at picking out a particular branch simply because you're so familiar with the setting. One of the problems with the scope, however, is that the higher the magnification, the harder it is to hold it steady on the object observed.

That's where a tripod comes in handy. If you have a place to keep a scope mounted near a window, it will be even more useful. Honesty urges me to add that whichever window it's close to *won't be the window from which you spot the bird.* The same principle holds true for binoculars or field glasses. Ours hang on a nail beside the west kitchen window. Birds unidentifiable with the naked eye are invariably sighted from the east kitchen window, unless someone has carelessly left the binoculars on the table beside it. It's a rule.

One other possibility is a monocular, which is essentially half of a binocular. Still prismatic, it's used by one eye only. Its drawback is that you can't achieve the three-dimensional quality you get with binoculars.

One word of caution about binoculars. Sometimes you'll find advertised what sounds like a great price. The ad may say "TEN TO FIFTY POWER MAGNIFICATION!" Read the fine print. If it says they're "non-prismatic," they're not really binoculars, no matter what they look like. Non-prismatic binoculars are a contradiction in terms. Binoculars aren't straight tubes. Those bumps contain the prisms. You'd be better off with good, optical quality field glasses or a telescope than with "non-prismatic" binoculars with molded or poured plastic lenses, and phony bumps.

COURSES IN IDENTIFICATION

Once equipped with field guide and binoculars, you might want to go one step further and take a course through adult education at a nearby school. If your interest continues to grow, you may be tempted to investigate local bird clubs. One way or another, you're all set to identify your guests. A lot of our fun in feeding birds consists of watching their behavior, and the field guides give few clues about that. If we're to have the chance to observe characteristic behavior, we'll also need to know just what foods to use to entice a particular species to the feeder. Discovering that preferences are for berries or insects or seeds just isn't enough. Which berries? What do I substitute for insects or won't those birds come to the feeder at all? What kind of seed?

Once you acquire the habit of looking closely at birds so that you can identify them by referring to your field guide, you'll discover that some of their physical characteristics provide clues to their behavior. Some of these physical attributes are related to the feeding behavior of birds. Take the size and shape of the bill. Seed eaters like sparrows and finches have short, stubby ones. Cardinals and grosbeaks, with their thicker, heavier bills, can handle larger seeds than, say, a goldfinch. The scissors-like bills of crossbills enable them to extract seeds from pine cones. Woodpeckers have strong bills, like chisels. Warblers and wrens, with their thin, sharply pointed bills, are primarily insect eaters. Birds of prey have hooked bills, ideally suited for tearing meat.

We've mentioned that birds seem to have color preferences and, in passing, pointed out that they have superb vision, perhaps the sharpest of any animal. Obviously that helps them locate food and contributes to their safety. The position of the eyes on the head is a hint to whether the bird is the hunter—hawks and owls look ahead—or the hunted—woodcocks and grouse have their eyes positioned more to the side and can see farther to the rear than can birds of prey.

Hearing is acute in birds too. Woodpeckers are thought to listen for insects, and owls rely on sound when hunting their prey. Experimental studies have determined the range of hearing in many species. Though many of us may have believed that robins locate earthworms by sound, ornithologists tend to think that the characteristic cocking of the head is related to visual hunting instead.

Look at the legs and feet of the birds you see for further clues to their habits: webbed feet for swimmers, long legs for waders, talons for birds of prey. Birds such as swallows and humming-

Mallards love corn and a quiet sanctuary.

birds that take their meals on the wing have small, weak feet. They can perch, but their feet aren't much good for anything else. What a contrast to the thrushes, which forage on the ground!

CHECK THE COLOR

Color is another hint about behavior. Ground dwellers tend to be duller in appearance than arboreal (tree-inhabiting) birds. Sparrows, which usually prefer to nest and forage on the ground, are brownish. Grosbeaks and finches, mostly brightly colored, are more active in trees. (There is evidence to suggest that the brightly colored birds aren't as tasty to hunters, either.) Females and juveniles generally tend to be less colorful than males even among arboreal species, doubtless another natural safety device to provide protection for incubating and other relatively helpless creatures.

There are over 8,500 *living* species of birds in the world, and it's estimated that the present bird population is about 100 billion. This continent itself has nearly 700 species in seventeen orders and over seventy families. We can't cover them all. Choices must

be made. No matter how that's done, somebody's favorite will get short shrift or be ignored completely. What I'll attempt to do is nod in the direction of the more common feeder birds to get you started. For convenience, there will be three chapters on bird families. The first will deal with perching birds, an order that contains more species than any other and whose members form the backbone of feeder society. The next chapter will include selected members of three orders that readily avail themselves of feeders: woodpeckers, pigeons and doves, and hummingbirds. The third will lump together three quite dissimilar kinds of birds that many people enjoy feeding but that present special problems: game birds, water birds, and birds of prey.

If the brief capsule accounts whet your appetite for complete biographies, help is at hand. In 1960, the highly respected John K. Terres started work on an encyclopedia of this continent's bird life, the heart of which is biographies of 847 species that breed or have been sighted in North America. The scope of the work is impressive indeed. The 1,109 pages of *The Audubon Society Encyclopedia of North American Birds* were finally published by Alfred A. Knopf in 1980. Twenty years were devoted to the project, and it represents our definitive study of birds. It is by no means the only work available, however. You'll be able to find impressive and/or entertaining bird lore whatever your area of greatest interest or your taste in reading material.

8
Most
Common
Feeder
Birds

Most of the birds we see at our feeders are members of the order *Passeriformes*, or perching birds. Indeed, the order contains more species than any other. All the birds in this order have four toes on each foot, three of them pointing forward and one pointing to the rear. The feet are never webbed, the better to facilitate perching. Their configuration is perfection itself for hanging onto a perch, in fact.

The young of the group are completely helpless when hatched. They're naked and blind. The parent birds care for them in the nest, usually until they're able to fly.

We'll ignore a number of common families among the perching birds because they don't normally come to feeders. Some are insect eaters exclusively; some have an extremely limited range. It's possible that we have numbers of them around our homes, but in many cases it's difficult to observe very much of their behavior up close. When members of a species take food on the wing rather than from a stationary feeding area, it's a lot more difficult for us to notice their interactions. Among the perching birds excluded, then, because we rarely see them at feeders, are phoebes, pewees, and other flycatchers, martins and other swallows, larks, shrikes, and pipits. You won't find dippers or vireos either. Within some of the families discussed, some species will be overlooked if they aren't typical feeder birds. Crows and ravens, for example, belong to the same family that jays do, but since they usually give feeders a wide berth, they aren't included. I'll limit myself to those birds you're most likely to see near the house. The families are covered, quite arbitrarily, in alphabetical order.

WAXWINGS

We begin with waxwings, the family *Bombycillidae*. There are only two species to consider, the Bohemian waxwing and the cedar waxwing. They're lovely brown birds, similar in appearance to each other and easy to recognize because both have crests and broad yellow bands at the tips of their tails. The Bohemian waxwing is the larger of the two, about the size of a robin, and the cedar waxwing is roughly an inch smaller. The cedar waxwing is far more common and can be observed over most of the continent

cedar waxwing

at one time or another. We'll confine our discussion to the cedars, sometimes called cherry birds, for that reason. Remember, though, that the habits of the two are quite similar.

Waxwings are primarily fruit eaters, and except during the nesting season, they live and travel in flocks numbering from about a dozen to over a hundred. Fortunately, they seem to prefer wild fruit to the domesticated kinds. Early cherries may be on their menu if native fruits haven't ripened, however. Though waxwings will come to feeders for fruit, many bird lovers rely on their gardens to feed these birds. They're fond of juniper berries, mountain ash, dates, cotoneaster, highbush cranberries, currants, the blossoms of blue gum eucalyptus, the buds of Chinese and Siberian elms, pyracantha berries, sand cherries, Japanese barberry, asparagus, birch seeds and buds, and Hopa crab apples. In our yard, they hang out in the honeysuckle bushes when the berries ripen, and they like our old apple tree. If you'd like them at your feeder as well as in your garden, entice them with raisins, apple slices, orange sections, and sunflower seeds. Both kinds of waxwings eat only a small percentage of animal food, mostly insects, but sometimes will sample meat scraps at a feeder. Like so many other birds, they find white bread an acceptable snack.

GREEDY OR GENEROUS?

One occasionally hears a hint of criticism about waxwings. It's whispered that they tend to gluttony. In the same breath, quite likely you'll hear praise for their gentle behavior and generosity. Their practice of lining up on a branch and passing a fruit or berry from one to the other all down the row and back again is well documented and seems to refute the slur on their appetites. It's possible that these apparently prodigious appetites are noticed primarily because the waxwings travel in flocks—that the bushes and trees are quickly stripped as a result of their numbers rather than because of greediness.

Waxwings migrate, but their distribution is such that some may be in evidence in most areas at almost any time of the year. The Bohemian waxwings prefer to nest in coniferous forests, the cedar waxwings in orchards, pines, or brushy borders.

BROWN CREEPERS

The family to which brown creepers belong, *Certhiidae,* occurs all over the northern part of the world. Creepers are smaller than a sparrow and are frequently overlooked because they blend so well with their usual background.

The creeper's usual background is a tree trunk, which he ascends in spirals to a height of about twenty feet and then flutters down to the next tree and starts all over again. He's after tiny insects and their eggs and larvae. His slender, curved bill is well suited for the occupation and his stiff tail serves as a prop. Creepers don't damage any crops, and their relentless search for insects yields dormant ones in winter as well as tiny ones that birds of the woodpecker tribe overlook. Except during their migrations, you're unlikely to see many creepers together at any given time. During the winter months they may feed with flocks of chickadees and nuthatches, on the fringes of the group. They're not particularly gregarious. They'll come to a feeder for suet, chopped peanuts, and occasionally white bread. They like peanut butter, which some people spread on the trunks of trees for the convenience of the little bird.

Creepers are most likely to be seen in winter except in the far north or in high altitudes. They're thought to be monogamous. Once it was believed that they were cavity nesters, but it's known now that the nests are built under loose bark still attached to the tree. Their activities are so restricted—up and down, up and down, searching trees for food—that they occasionally behave peculiarly. If, during their travels, they reach a treeless area, they'll creep up any vertical object available, whether it be a fence post, telegraph pole, or brick wall.

THE NOISY SET

The family *Corvidae*, of which crows, jays, and magpies are members, is not likely to be overlooked. Some of these birds are strikingly handsome; all are conspicuous.

Crows are, perhaps, the best-known bird on the continent. Often maligned, they're easily tamed and intelligent, and they make good pets. Occasionally they come to feeders (they especially like bread), but few of us encourage them. For one thing, a crow needs about a pound and a half of food daily. They prefer to eat on the ground, which is just as well, considering their size. While there is no reason to persecute these birds, neither is there need to encourage them. They're capable of fending for themselves under most conditions. Despite the campaigns that have been waged against them, they're probably more numerous now than when the colonists arrived.

Magpies, just about crow-sized, are striking black and white western birds seldom seen at feeders. Clark's nutcrackers are well-known jay-sized gray and black birds of the western mountains. Practically a tourist attraction in the Rockies, they're fond of meat and peanuts, which will lure them to feeders in their range. They have acquired a reputation as camp robbers. Like the gray jay, or "Whiskey Jack," they're both bold and inquisitive—and quite willing to engage in thievery.

Clark's nutcracker has been the subject of research on animal memory. Like other *Corvidae* family members, it stores food, and psychologists have discovered that the birds remember where they put it. Apparently they make clusters of caches and utilize large landmarks as reminders. They clean out one batch before starting on another.

TWO CRESTED JAYS

Our two crested jays are the blue jay and Steller's jay. Generally speaking, their ranges don't overlap. The blue-and-white blue jay occurs east of the Rockies, the black-and-blue Steller's jay from the Rockies westward. Both are, for all practical purposes, omnivorous, and both come readily to feeders, where they tend to drive other birds away. Since they're quick to discover new food sources, they frequently are among the early arrivals at a freshly installed feeder.

Most people never have a chance to hear any of the soft, melodic songs of jay but are quick to recognize their less mellifluous shrieks and jeers. Their cries frequently alert other wildlife to the presence of danger.

BLUE JAY

Blue jays are abundant in their range, in yards with or without feeders, in parks and any other places they may find scraps left by picnickers. They also are road-kill scavengers. They tend to feed earlier in the day than many of the other feeder birds, and they

blue jay

prefer ground feeding. Swinging feeders discourage them. Their food preferences are bread, corn, peanuts, nutmeats, suet, and sunflower seeds. They aren't fond of the smaller seeds. Plant food supplies 90 percent of their needs in winter and 60 percent in summer. To the fruits, berries, and nuts in season, they'll add ants, snails, and small fish and frogs.

I miss the blue jays while they are busy during the summer raising their families (and, some say, preying on other nests). Along about August we start hearing their cries, and shortly the impudent, good-looking rascals are at the feeders again, commenting derisively on our offerings. It's probably a character fault that makes me enjoy their foibles so thoroughly.

In the East, blue jays have served as experimental subjects. (It's significant, I think, of this family's reputation for intelligence that they're used in this way.) They have demonstrated, to the satisfaction of one researcher at least, an ability to concentrate. No one who has watched them around the garden is apt to deny it.

STELLER'S JAY

Steller's jays like nuts, acorns, and fruit. Sometimes their appetite for fruit gets them into trouble with orchardists. Like blue jays, they have the reputation of occasionally eating the eggs and nestlings of smaller birds. In an effort to dissuade them, don't forget to offer them eggshells at the feeding station, along with the bread, crackers, and meat scraps they'll devour so eagerly.

OTHER JAYS

Gray jays, also called Oregon jays and Canada jays, are common in northern woods and mountainous areas. They have no crest and resemble large, disheveled chickadees. They're also called "Whiskey Jacks," "meat birds," and several other names, some of them unprintable. Inveterate thieves, they steal food from camps and bait or game from traps. Like other jays, they often take away more food than they can eat and store it. They're especially partial to baked beans and meat, raw or cooked. They're as willing to take these goodies from a camper's table as from a feeding tray.

Some authorities call the scrub jay the Florida jay and assert that it is found only in Florida. Others claim that it is found also in the chaparral country of the West. Still another group insists that it's the same species as Woodhouse's jay. It is a crestless bird, blue and gray with no white markings. It's not quite as strident in voice as other jays. Scrub jays feed on acorns, peas, corn, grain, and nuts as well as ants, wasps, and other animal food. They'll come to feeders and especially like bread, peanuts, and suet. They tame easily.

The pinyon jay, our only dull-blue jay, is a western bird of foothills and croplands. Like the others, it's omnivorous, but its name suggests its favorite food. A correspondent of mine in North Dakota regards pinyon jays as nuisances at the feeders because they come "in hordes" to devour sunflower seeds.

One of the gaudier jays, the green jay, is found only in southern Texas. Before the practice of selling wild birds as pets became illegal, it was much in demand as a cage bird because of its brilliant plumage. It's green with a crestless blue cap, black throat, black bill, and yellow outer tail feathers. It seems fond of corn and meat and is known to raid garbage cans. It has been reported to enter kitchens and take food from plates, so it can't be considered significantly different in temperament from other jays.

THE LARGEST FAMILY

Our next family of birds is *Fringillidae*, the largest family of birds known. Some ornithologists refer to the *Fringillidae* as the sparrow family; some refer to it as the finch family; the cagey ones (including Peterson) refer to it as the family of grosbeaks, finches, sparrows, and buntings. The most common characteristic of the family is the bill. It is short and stout, adapted to seed-eating. These birds eat insects, fruits, and berries also, but their staple item of diet is seeds. The sparrows, primarily terrestrial, are mostly brown birds with little difference between the sexes in coloration. The grosbeaks, finches, and buntings are often colorful, females and males usually distinctively different in plumage.

CARDINAL

We'll begin with what may well be the most popular of all our native birds, the cardinal. The most casual observer is pleased by sighting our only crested red bird. Cardinals are usually listed with grosbeaks because of their very heavy bills. The female is much more subdued in appearance than the male but still easily recognized. Cardinals are usually seen in pairs, and sometimes two or more pairs visit the same feeding stations. The species, a non-migratory one, was formerly considered a southern bird, but it has vastly extended its range northward. We have a couple of pairs coming regularly to our feeders here in western Massachusetts, and friends in Iowa boast six or eight at a time. We see them most often at the honeysuckle bush during its fruiting season. Cardinals also like the hornbeam, and my Aunt Vi in Illinois has counted eleven males and five females at one time enjoying the catkins on

cardinal

her birch in January. Friends in West Virginia feed shelled peanuts to cardinals from their back porch every evening. If Kate and Bud are late in appearing, the birds fly to the kitchen window to remind them.

Many people know that cardinals are fond of sunflower seeds. These birds also like watermelon and cantaloupe seeds, scratch feed, bread, and peanut butter. Though they'll feed on the ground, they don't mind a hanging or stationary feeder. In the yard, cardinals will feast on almonds, white ash, American elm, and both cherry and autumn elaeagnus, as well as blackberries and honeysuckle berries, and the seeds of four o'clocks. If you live in a subtropical climate, you may have discovered that they dote on camphor trees. Though cardinals are basically seed and fruit eaters, such insects as ants and beetles may account for up to a third of their food when available.

GROSBEAKS

Having started out with cardinals, sometimes called cardinal grosbeaks, we will move on to other grosbeaks. The evening grosbeak has also extended its range, much more dramatically, in fact, than the cardinal. This boldly colored yellow bird with black and white wings was once rare except in the Northwest. Since the turn of the century it has become increasingly widely distributed and now winters regularly as far south as the Washington-Baltimore area on a line extending westward through Ohio. Some individuals nest as far south as New Jersey. Grosbeaks have been reported in all of the contiguous forty-eight states, including northern Florida and Louisiana.

With their powerful bills, evening grosbeaks are able to extract the kernels of large seeds. Some people consider them pests because of their gluttony, but it's probably more common for those who stock feeders to report their appetites with a kind of awe. Though they're willing to eat most seeds, they are especially fond of sunflower seeds, peanuts, and safflower seeds. Away from the feeder, they eat both buds and seeds of box elders, which are widely planted from the Plains States to the East. Cottonwoods and catalpas also attract them, as well as white ash, elm, beech, maple, dogwood, sumac, and honeysuckle. Their diet is nearly all of vegetable origin, but in the summer they dine on some insects and feed considerable numbers to nestlings. They prefer conifers as nesting sites. They're gregarious birds and customarily live in good-sized flocks. Even when nesting, they aren't strongly territorial, although usually there's but one nest to a tree.

The grosbeaks are all handsome birds. The females are much drabber in appearance, probably for safety while incubating the eggs. The female rose-breasted grosbeak, for example, is brown and streaked like a sparrow, but the male is unmistakable—black and white with a triangular red patch on his breast. They rarely come to feeders but are attracted to barberry, beech trees, corn, cherries, and redbud, and they are reputed to have a truly admirable appetite for the Colorado potato beetle. In range the rose-breasted grosbeak is far more restricted than the evening grosbeak, breeding from the Plains States to the Northeast and south to Georgia and Appalachia. It swings far north and west of the Plains States in Canada, however.

BLACK-HEADED GROSBEAK

The western counterpart of the rose-breasted grosbeak is the black-headed grosbeak, also known as the western grosbeak, which is remarkably similar in song and quiet temperament but not as brilliant in plumage. Its fondness for early fruit, peas, and beans is balanced by its consumption of scale insects (about a fourth of its diet), beetles, canker worms, and snails. Although its diet is more than two-thirds animal in origin, it will visit feeders for white bread and butter or sunflower seeds.

PINE GROSBEAK

The pine grosbeak is reddish with white wingbars. Altogether it reminds one of a very large purple finch. It's fairly widely distributed over the northern part of the continent and extends south to

Mexico in western coniferous forests. Almost all of its diet is vegetable. Although it rarely visits feeders, it will be happy to dine in your garden if you can supply apples, sumac, maples, willows, ash, blackberries, or grapes. The blue grosbeak tends more to the southern portion of the United States. Both birds consume some insects we consider harmful. Blue grosbeaks are sometimes cursed for invading grainfields for sorghum, oats, and corn. Blackberries and sunflowers are also apt to attract them. Gardeners are often willing to forgive them their occasional lapses because they're fond of crabgrass seed.

FINCHES

Perhaps the best known of the numerous finches is the American goldfinch or "wild canary," found in numbers all over the continental United States. Although there is a discernible shift of population in winter, goldfinches remain within their normal range all year. Their diet is nearly all seeds. At the feeder they'll eat thistle, hemp, millet, sunflower seeds, and nutmeats, but they are just as happy with the seeds of garden flowers and weeds. Among their favorites are wild thistle, catnip, coreopsis, dandelion, and cosmos. They also like goldenrod, hornbeam, birch, larch, and Chinese and Siberian elms. They won't nest where there isn't a good supply of wild thistle. Not only do they feed on its seeds, but they also use the down of the seedpod to line their nests.

There are good reasons why most of us feel drawn to goldfinches. We probably associate them with pet birds, as witness their common name. They're conspicuous because of their easily recognizable, attractive plumage and because they're usually found in numbers. When feeding, they seem almost ridiculously tame. They visit our flowers as soon as the seeds begin to ripen and rise in clouds when we walk past, but they don't go far, nor do they seem alarmed. I've often felt some fear for them feeding so close to the ground because of our extremely large local cat population, but they must have an effective communications network; I've observed no casualties. Their movements are quick; they're among the competent birds that steal choice tidbits from other birds at feeders.

The varied and melodic song of the goldfinch elicits widespread praise. It's difficult, indeed, to uncover any criticism of the bird. In the winter, the coloring of the male becomes much paler, but that's hardly a cause for fault-finding. During the colder months they're apt to be found in the company of other small finches such as redpolls and pine siskins, which they somewhat resemble.

The lesser goldfinch (formerly called the Arkansas goldfinch) is smaller, as you might expect, and is found only from Colorado west. The European goldfinch was introduced to America in 1852, multiplied very slowly, and seems to be disappearing. Lawrence's goldfinch is found only in California and (in winter) Arizona. It is strictly vegetarian.

American goldfinch

redpoll

REDPOLL

The common redpoll is not quite as widely distributed as the American goldfinch, its range being more northerly. Its diet is composed entirely of plant food. Birch and alder are its favorite seeds, but it also likes dandelion, ragweed, and catalpa seeds. At feeders it likes rolled oats, hemp, millet, and sunflower seeds.

PINE SISKIN

Pine siskins, the most common winter finch, are considered erratic nomads. Found all over the country, they'll visit your feeder if they're in the neighborhood. They show aggressive behavior at feeders, and are not above stealing seeds from other birds. If you serve millet, hemp, nutmeats, or sunflower seeds, be prepared for

pine siskin

droves of these finches. Apart from feeder treats, they like birch seeds and buds, alder, and Scotch thistle.

PURPLE FINCH

Purple finches and house finches are closely related and similar in appearance. The former are more widely distributed and tend to prefer forests, while house finches like arid, open country. I've heard it said that purple finches have not established the friendly relationship with humans that house finches have, a statement that astonishes me. Our feeders are filled with purple finches all summer long, with somewhat fewer in winter. They like squash and pumpkin seeds, bread, scratch feed, millet, hemp, nutmeats, and sunflower seeds. Among the landscape plants they feed on are ash, American elm, birch, beech, box elder, balsam fir, spruce, Amur honeysuckle, privet, butternut, cotoneaster, and smoketree.

Most of my friends report numbers of purple finches at their feeders. They will use trays, hoppers, or swinging feeders with equal enthusiasm. If they feel I'm tardy in refilling a feeder, they tell me about it. They allow me to approach very close before they retreat to a nearby tree or bush. Sometimes I see large numbers of them, often in the company of goldfinches and house sparrows, foraging on the ground near the feeders.

HOUSE FINCH

House finches are a western bird. They were illegally introduced into New York City about forty years ago as cage birds. When the dealers discovered their legal peril, they released the finches, which now thrive from eastern Connecticut to the Midwest to the deep South, as well as in their normal western range. Recently some have been reported in Massachusetts, so the expansion seems to be still in progress. Their native haunts are Mexico, southwestern United States, and California north to British Columbia. They're also found in Hawaii, though no one is certain how they got there. Interestingly, there are regional differences in the birds. In humid areas their plumage is darker; in the desert it's very bright. The eastern birds, for reasons so far unexplained, have shorter tails, wings, legs, and toes and bigger bills than their western relatives. They're also said to exhibit less variety in song. House finches aren't fussy about nesting sites and sometimes use the abandoned homes of other birds. They are extremely abundant in their normal range and, as their name suggests, have readily adapted to human settlements.

The bills of house finches attest to their food preference—seeds—but they've acquired a bad reputation among fruit growers because they frequent orchards, where their numbers make them a problem. One writer reported that house finches that had gorged on rotting peaches in her garden became quite silly in behavior. At feeders, they hold their own even against house sparrows. They prefer sunflower seeds above other feeder fare but are willing to make do with hemp, millet, cracked corn, fruits, bread, peanuts, and suet.

SPARROWS

We've been considering the brightly colored birds of the *Fringillidae* tribe. For a change of pace, we turn now to the sparrows. They offer a real problem in identification to the novice. There are so many different kinds, such subtle differences. We'll just mention those that rarely come to feeders: Bachman's, Cape Sable, clay-colored, grasshopper, Henslow's, Ipswich, lark, Le Conte's, Lincoln's, savannah, seaside, sharp-tailed, swamp, vesper—and "dusky" seaside. Of the last, there are five known left in the world and they live in Gainesville, Florida, in a zoo. All five are males, which does not bode well for the future of their species.

SONG SPARROW

We'll begin with the song sparrow, found all over the country but varying considerably according to local environmental conditions (at least twenty-five subspecies have been described).

Most song sparrows migrate south of their nesting areas in winter, but not very far, and not for long. They're largely terrestrial,

chipping sparrow

song sparrow

and their colorings reflect their habits. They're identified by heavily streaked underparts forming a dark blotch in the middle of the breast. Although not as adaptable to close contact with people as the chipping sparrow, their sweet and varied songs have made the song sparrows well loved. They'll come to feeders for hemp and millet, bread and doughnut crumbs, and peanut butter. Occasionally they sample suet and cracked corn. They prefer feeding on the ground on fallen or scattered seed but will learn to use hanging or stationary feeders. Blackberries, raspberries, and elderberries will provide nesting sites as well as food for them. Nestlings are fed mostly insects or larvae found on or near the ground. By wintertime, about 90 percent of the song sparrow's diet is vegetable, consisting largely of seeds, especially weed seeds.

CHIPPING SPARROW

The chipping sparrow is sometimes called the "social sparrow" because it's tame in the manner of robins. It adapted readily to our growing population but was for some time threatened by the imported house sparrows. The chipping sparrow rapidly expanded its population with the decline in numbers of house sparrows. Although found in the West, it is most common in the eastern United States. Its nest, when horses were more numerous, was usually lined with horsehair. It is frequently victimized by cow-birds. Chipping sparrows feed on insects, plant seeds, and, occasionally, berries. At the feeder, they'll take bread, cracked corn, millet, oats, peanut butter, and suet. You'll recognize the slender bird by its gray breast, reddish cap, forked tail, and white eye stripe.

TREE SPARROW

The tree sparrow also has a reddish cap but is distinguished from the chipping sparrow by the black spot on its breast. Tree sparrows are found over most of the country but are more abundant along the Pacific Coast. During the winter they're often seen at feeders, where they're relatively tame. They will peck at suet, and they also like bread, cracked corn, hemp, peanut butter, and pumpkin seeds. Their natural food consists of weed and grass seeds and, in summer, a few insects.

FIELD SPARROW

The field sparrow is primarily an eastern sparrow. He's similar in appearance to the tree sparrow, but without the black spot on his breast. Field sparrows commonly flock with chipping sparrows and like essentially the same feeder tidbits: cracked corn, corn bread, proso millet, peanut butter, and suet. Their natural food is primarily the seeds of grass and weeds; in summer they add many insects to their diet, such as tent caterpillars, beetles, ants, and flies.

tree sparrow

field sparrow

FOX SPARROW

The fox sparrow, so called because of its reddish hue, is a large sparrow and perhaps the easiest one to recognize. He's found all over the continental United States and has a larger number of subspecies than any other sparrow except the song sparrow. Fox sparrows eat weed seeds, birch and alder, wild fruit, the berries of holly, euonymus, and cedar, and insects. At the feeder, they'll accept millet, cracked corn, and suet. They're more likely to come in times of heavy snow cover than in open weather.

HARRIS'S SPARROW

Harris's sparrow is common to the Great Plains. It is our largest sparrow, distinctive in appearance, with black cap, face, and bib. In nature its food is mostly weed and grass seeds, although it likes some fruits, such as cranberries. It will take corn, sunflower seeds, hemp, or wheat on the ground or at window feeders. Another sparrow, the white-crowned, is found more often in the West. Its very rarity makes it highly esteemed by eastern bird feeders. In summer its diet is largely insects, but at other seasons it becomes a weed and grass seed eater, supplemented with waste grain and wild fruit. At feeders it likes bread crumbs, cracked corn, sunflower seeds, and walnut meats. The white-throated sparrow is more apt to be found in the eastern portion of the country, where it thrives on insects, berries, and weed seeds. At the feeder it prefers peanut hearts and cracked corn. It is adept at the art of thievery.

Because sparrows nest and forage on and near the ground, they're subject to certain dangers usually avoided by more arboreal birds. For example, they are among the prey of bullfrogs (which, in turn, may be the prey of crows, grackles, and owls). The young develop very rapidly and often leave the nest before they're able to fly. The male takes over feeding chores while the female gets busy on another brood. Both the chipping sparrow and the field sparrow have an interesting characteristic as nestlings, perhaps a throwback to their reptilian origins: they are cold-blooded when hatched. Both sparrows become warm-blooded by the age of seven days.

JUNCOS

About the general size and shape of the sparrows is that gregarious group known as juncos, or snowbirds. They always have white outer tail feathers and a white belly. The rest of their plumage is gray or black, without streaks, but sometimes rufous or pinkish on the sides. They hybridize readily with one another (and, very occasionally, with white-throated sparrows), so they are quite variable, and many subspecies have been named. We'll content ourselves with the three major juncos.

THREE JUNCOS

The most widely distributed is the slate-colored junco. At one time or another, it's found all over the United States, but it breeds mostly in Alaska, Canada, and New England, south through mountainous areas to Georgia. It prefers feeding on the ground, its favorite feeder foods being bread, cracked corn, peanuts, millet, suet, sunflower seeds, and wheat. In the summertime juncos thrive on ants, spiders, caterpillars, and grasshoppers, in addition to weed and grass seeds and a few wild berries. Except during the breeding season, juncos are usually found in flocks; the average number in a flock is sixteen. They associate not only with other juncos but also with towhees, myrtle warblers, and fox and white-throated sparrows during the winter.

junco

Snow is a problem to these hardy little birds when it covers their natural food. At such times, flocks are likely to wander extensively in search of bare ground. They've been sighted on coastal beaches during periods of heavy snow cover.

The Oregon junco, formerly called the pink-sided junco, looks much like the slate-colored junco except that the back is brown and the sides pinkish. It's common in the western United States but is sighted only rarely east of the Great Plains, usually in the company of other juncos. Like the slate-colored juncos, it likes bread and small grains, scattered on the ground.

The range of the white-winged junco is rather limited, occurring mostly in pine-forested mountains from the Great Plains west. Slightly larger and paler than the slate-colored junco, it has two distinct wing bars and more white in its tail. Its habits and voice are quite similar to the other juncos and it is likely to be found with them in mixed flocks.

Although it's theoretically possible for many feeders of birds to attract all three of the major categories of juncos, in practice it's unlikely except in the Great Plains area. My correspondent in South Dakota reports having all three regularly all winter long. Wherever juncos are found, they're welcome visitors, attractive and well mannered.

BUNTINGS

Let's move on to something a bit smaller but a great deal more flamboyant, the buntings. The most distinctive, the male painted bunting, has a purple head, green back, and red breast. It was once a popular cage bird because of its spectacular plumage. Pugnacious about territory, it was easy to trap for sale, using a dummy or stuffed bird as a lure. The female is green, the only native finch that can claim that distinction. Painted buntings are found from North Carolina west to Kansas and thence south. They feed on weed and grass seeds, pine seeds, sunflower seeds, and rice, as well as flies, wasps, and boll weevils. Insects account

painted bunting

for about a quarter of their diet. At feeders they eat mixed seeds, peanut hearts, cracked corn, and bread crumbs. They nest in elms, oaks, and blackberry bushes. They're considered shy.

INDIGO AND LAZULI BUNTINGS

The indigo bunting, far more abundant, breeds throughout the United States from the Great Plains east, excluding southern Florida and southern Texas. It's the only native bird that is dark blue all over. Your first sighting of an indigo bunting is apt to leave you gasping with disbelief: they're astonishingly brilliant. Because they like brush, young second growth, orchards, and pastures, they're much more common now than they were during colonial times. They seem to enjoy the heat of the day in July and August, singing persistently when other birds retire to trees and thickets. They eat blackberries, corn, and dandelion seeds as well as beetles and caterpillars. Sometimes they come to feeders for wheat or nutmeats, and they may be attracted to a birdbath. They nest both in maples and briar patches.

The lazuli bunting is the western counterpart of the indigo bunting, occurring from the Great Plains to the Pacific Coast, except in Texas. Their ranges overlap and the two hybridize so regularly that some ornithologists believe they should be treated as one species. Where the range doesn't overlap, however, the plumage is distinctly different. The lazuli bunting has white wing bars and a chestnut breast. Some birders believe them to be wary of humans, and they are rare visitors to feeding stations. If they are common in your area, you might try attracting them with the foods that indigo buntings enjoy.

SNOW BUNTING

The snow bunting is nowhere common at feeders, and if we see it at all in the North it will be in winter. It is our whitest land bird. The male has black feathers on back, wings, and tail; the female is similar, with rusty instead of black markings. At seven inches, it's larger than the other buntings. It feeds on amaranth, corn, wheat, and barley, supplemented by beetles and caterpillars in season. Encountering one in your garden can be considered a *coup*. Scatter some cracked corn or oats to please these rare visitors.

CROSSBILLS

The crossbills are among the strangest looking of our native birds. The peculiar crossing of the mandibles enables them to get to the seeds of conifers and apples in short order. They're sparrow-sized birds. The red crossbill is dull red with black wings and tail; the white-winged is lighter, almost pink, and has white wing bars. Both of them are, not surprisingly, partial to coniferous forests, especially spruce forests, but the red crossbill has a much wider range. It may be attracted to your property by American beech, almonds, balsam firs, hemlock, pine, and sumac. At feeders it prefers sunflower seeds above other seeds. The range of the white-winged crossbill is restricted to the northern tier of states, but it too has been reported at feeders. Both are reputedly fond of salt, salt water, or a mixture of mud and salt.

PYRRHULOXIA

The *Fringillidae* family member I'd most like to encounter is the pyrrhuloxia. It's medium-sized—eight or nine inches—and looks something like a cross between a parrot and a cardinal. Found only in our Southwest, it's been called the gray cardinal and the bullfinch, among other common names. Generally, the bird is gray with red crest, tail, breast, chin, and throat. It feeds

pyrrhuloxia

on insects and weed seeds and can be lured to feeders with kitchen scraps. If I lived in its home area, I'd do my best to attract this exotic creature.

DICKCISSEL

The dickcissel causes a great commotion in the birder's world because it is irregular in its habits. At one time, for example, it was quie common along the Atlantic seaboard, but then it disappeared entirely in that area. (It may be making a comeback now.) Though it's fairly abundant in the Midwest, its appearance even there is sporadic. It isn't known whether these population fluctuations are a result of diseases or migration disasters.

The dickcissel is an attractive bird of sparrow size with streaked brown back, yellow breast, and black bib. It's considered a beneficial bird because it has more interest in insect food than most finches, consuming crickets, ants, flies, and the like to account for about four-fifths of its diet. It will visit feeders for peanut butter, millet, oats, wheat, and corn. Typically it nests in elm, mulberry, or Osage orange trees. Dickcissels are early migrators, packing up in August immediately after the nesting season is over and heading for South America in flocks of 200 or 300 birds.

TOWHEES

We'll finish up the *Fringillidae* with some birds less eye-catching than the pyrrhuloxia, but still handsome: the towhees, familiarly known as chewinks—to say nothing of swamp robin, ground robin, marsh robin, bullfinch, bushbird, and turkey sparrow. The fact that its more common names come from its call, which is transliterated both as towhee` and chewink`, may help clarify my distrust of written descriptions of bird songs. The same call has been written as joree-ziee, t'wee, shrink, and cherwink. Its song is variously written as "Drink your tea, see towhee" and "Sweet bird sing" and "Cheet, cheet, cheer" and "Cheap, cheap cheese." Some of these variations may be a result of differences in songs and calls in different parts of the country, but even so, they strike me as less than helpful.

SEVERAL SPECIES

Several different species and subspecies of towhees have been described, including eastern, spotted, green-tailed, Abert's, canyon, Oregon, rileyi, white-eyed, and brown towhees. Somewhat later these were simply lumped into two species, the eastern and the western towhee. Since about 1957, however, many ornithologists have insisted that there is only *one* towhee, and that the variations in plumage are a result of environmental factors. So we'll talk about generalities, and then point out the more obvious differences to be found in towhees scattered over the continent.

Towhees are roughly robin-sized. They nest on or near the ground, and the female is apt to perform the injured-wing routine if you surprise her on or near the nest. If you're simply in the vicinity, she'll leave the nest and, when she judges herself to be a safe distance away, attempt some activity to draw attention to herself. Cowbirds frequently choose towhee nests for parasitizing. If more than two or three cowbird eggs are deposited, the towhee deserts the nest, apparently realizing that she's been had.

Towhees eat spiders and snails, ants, beetles, flies, wasps, grasshoppers, and caterpillars as part of their diet. In addition, they feed on seeds, wild fruits and berries, and mast. They're ground feeders. To lure them to your feeding area, use pieces of shelled peanuts, nutmeats, cracked corn, and sunflower and watermelon seeds. They dote on the crumbs of bread, crackers, and dough-

towhee

nuts, and they love to bathe in birdbaths. They'll gather in the sumac in your "natural" area and may be found dining on raspberries, blackberries, blueberries, and strawberries. You'll know their location because they make a terrific racket, scratching like domestic chickens.

The eastern race of towhees is frequently referred to as rufous-sided towhees. Males have white breasts, black heads, backs, and wings, and robin-colored sides. White spots in the tail are conspicuous in flight and there are white markings on the wing. In the female, black is replaced with brown. These birds are found, at one season or another, from coast to coast. A slightly smaller western variation, with considerably more white on the wings and some on the back, is called the spotted towhee or the Oregon towhee. The Southwest and California have a brown towhee. The green-tailed towhee, found from the Great Plains west, is even smaller. The edges and underparts of the wing are yellow, the cap rufous (reddish), the throat white.

LONGSPURS

Before we leave the *Fringillidae*, I will briefly mention the longspurs, sparrow-like birds not often seen at feeders since they're primarily birds of open country. If severe weather drives them to your yard, they'll eat cracked corn.

BLACKBIRDS

The *Fringillidae* family includes some of the most sought-after feeder birds. On the other hand, the *Icteridae*, or blackbirds generally, have very few members considered highly desirable, though it would be hard to deny that they're a handsome group of birds.

COWBIRD

I can't think of a single common bird with a worse reputation than the cowbird. And you know how it is once anybody gets a bad reputation. All kinds of villainy, justified or not, are attributed to cowbirds. The source of the outrage is that cowbirds choose to leave the care of their offspring, from egg to adult, to some other species.

Here's what happens. The male cowbird, about robin-sized, black with a brown head, mates with the gray female; when she feels the urge to lay an egg, she scouts around for a nest to put it in. Something like 206 species have been recipients of her eggs, including such unlikely victims as hawks and gulls (the efforts failed, in those cases). The most usual targets are nests of vireos, warblers, sparrows, and flycatchers. All's well (for the cowbirds) if the female victim has finished laying and is about to start incubating. If, however, the nest is empty, the female of the host species is likely to desert it upon finding the cowbird eggs. Yellow warblers are likely to take a different tack: they build a new nest on top of the old one, even if one or two warbler eggs are in it. Nests as high as *six* stories have been found, the floor of each new nest covering a cowbird egg. Should the cowbird choose the nest of a robin or a catbird, her egg will promptly be punctured and/or tossed out.

If the female cowbird has chosen a nest carefully, her egg will probably hatch before the eggs of the victim, because cowbird eggs need only ten days' incubation. The young cowbird then gets the full attention of his foster parents. Should any of the other eggs hatch, the cowbird nestling, larger and more vigorous, will smother or destroy them. By the time he leaves the nest, he's often twice the size of the birds feeding him.

However indignant this behavior makes you feel, it might be sensible to consider a statement in *Audubon Bird Guide*, by Richard H. Pough (Garden City, New York: Doubleday and Company, Inc., 1949) *sponsored by* National Audubon Society: "But since the birds they most frequently impose upon continue to be about as abundant as their habitats permit, it is evident that the cowbird does not have an appreciable effect upon their population level."

In keeping with their tarnished reputation, cowbirds were once actually accused of being proponents of "free love." It has been determined that they are monogamous for the length of the breeding season, as are most perching birds

Cowbirds were formerly called buffalo birds because they used the beasts as beaters to stir up insects, which they consumed.

red-winged blackbird

cowbird

Adaptable creatures, as bison disappeared, cowbirds turned their attention to cattle. Cowbirds are found most frequently around farms, pastures, and open woodlands, over most of the United States. In addition to grasshoppers, leaf hoppers, and spiders, they eat grains, seeds, and berries. Except during the breeding season, they normally travel in flocks.

Most people don't try to attract cowbirds to feeders. Quite aside from our tendency to disapprove of their domestic arrangements, they consume a lot of feed. They especially like hemp, millet, scratch feed, and sunflower seeds, served on the ground, but then so do many birds people are eager to attract. Besides, cowbirds aren't fussy and will take almost anything they can get. To their credit, they're not aggressive but feed amicably with other birds. It may be, because of their appetite and numbers, that you'll decide you don't especially want to attract them, but surely it's not necessary to follow the lead of earlier bird lovers and actively try to exterminate them.

Bronzed cowbirds found from central Texas and Arizona south victimize fifty-two species, including finches and blackbirds, but especially orioles. Their habits are similar to those of brown-headed cowbirds. Another close relative in the same area is the red-eyed cowbird.

RED-WINGED BLACKBIRDS

Red-winged blackbirds are found all over the continental United States. They're handsome birds and easy to recognize. Red-winged blackbirds are extremely gregarious, even nesting in colonies. The males defend the small territory around their nests with vigor, however. Against intruders of other species, whether bird or mammal, red-winged blackbirds are ruthless. Many birds will dive at humans, but the redwings will strike as well. The nesting site is usually a marshy area, and the colony will range from a few pairs of birds to hundreds. After the nesting season, they gather in flocks and use communal roosts, often joined by grackles and starlings. Because of their numbers, they are sometimes a nuisance to farmers. Sometimes, especially in the southern states, the roosting grounds contain millions of birds. Generally, their food consists of about a quarter insects and three-quarters seeds and grains, including barley, rice, white ash, American beech, and cabbage palmetto. In summer as much as half of their diet may consist of ants, beetles, grasshoppers, snails, and spiders. They prefer to eat on the ground.

Though red-winged blackbirds move southward for the winter, they don't go far—or for very long—and a few will stay through the winter and visit feeding stations. This can be a mixed blessing, since they're large, aggressive, and possessed of vigorous appetites. They like practically everything: hemp, millet, cracked corn, raisins, apples, dog food (dry or wet), bread, doughnuts, and peanuts.

RUSTY BLACKBIRD

The rusty blackbird is found mainly from the Great Plains east, and Brewer's blackbird from the Great Plains west. Their ranges overlap considerably, especially in the South. The rusty is more a bird of the marshes and Brewer's a bird of fields and farmyards. Both somewhat resemble common grackles in appearance but are smaller, with shorter tails. Although Brewer's is fond of bread, neither is considered a feeder bird. Nor is the flashy yellow-headed blackbird, but grain scattered on the ground may attract it. Its diet is a third insects, the rest grain and seeds. It's generally found from the Great Plains west. Because these four blackbirds tend to occur in large numbers, their welcome at feeding stations is doubtful.

GRACKLES

Purple and bronzed grackles, which hybridize freely wherever their ranges overlap, are now considered subspecies of the common grackle rather than separate species. The purple or blue-green subspecies is more likely to be found in the South and East, the bronzed west of the Alleghenies. They're not usually found west of the Great Plains.

Grackles are larger than robins, about the size of blue jays. Superficially they resemble crows, but their smaller size and keeled tail make them readily identifiable. Their ability to adapt to changes wrought by civilization has enabled them to increase in numbers despite changing conditions. Once they were largely birds of the marshes, but they've invaded farmland, suburbs, parks, and urban areas. They're often among the first to discover a new feeding station, and they're quite capable of taking over. Competent thieves themselves, they seem to object violently when they're victimized by other birds. At the feeder, they'll take whatever is on the menu, but they're particularly partial to bread, corn, suet, nutmeats, sunflower seed, and wheat. If the bread products happen to be hard, they're apt to take them to the birdbath to dunk them before eating them.

Among the landscape plants that appeal especially to grackles are American beech and cabbage palmetto. Corn and wheat are their favorite cultivated grains, which they start raiding in July and August. After harvest, they rely on waste grain, weed seeds, and animal matter. Most of them migrate south and sometimes hang around barnyards in flocks to steal grain from domestic livestock.

Grackles eat animal food too; house sparrows, an occasional egg or nestling, or sometimes a field mouse. In the early spring they hunt small crustaceans and insects in marshes, and when plowing starts, they have a field day with the turned-up insects. Once it was thought that they hung around after seeds sprouted for the purpose of wreaking havoc on the young plants (that's what the wrong image can do for you), but it has since been determined that they're actually after cutworms. They feed their nestlings exclusively on insects and they eat more Japanese beetle grubs than any other bird. They're not totally devoid of usefulness after all.

BOAT-TAILED GRACKLE

The boat-tailed grackle is much larger, almost crow-sized, with an enormous tail. It's never found very far from water. Its range extends from New Jersey south to all of Florida and across the southern coast to Arizona. Its natural food is two-thirds grain and the rest mainly crustaceans. It comes to feeders for grain, meat scraps, and bread.

ORIOLES

Finally we come to the royal branch of the *Icteridae* family, the orioles. The American orioles are not related to European orioles. Their common name was the result of error, but it is now too firmly entrenched to change it. The Baltimore or northern and orchard orioles are found from the Great Plains east, Bullock's oriole from the Great Plains west. As sometimes happens, birds wander out of their accustomed range. Verified reports of both orchard and Baltimore orioles have been recorded in California.

Certain other orioles—hooded, black-headed and spotted-breasted among them—occur only in extremely limited ranges in south Texas, southern Florida, southern Arizona, and southwestern California. All of the orioles normally winter south of the United States. They are not common feeder birds during cold weather, but if for some reason they stay in their nesting areas, they will come readily to feeders. Baltimore orioles will often come to a feeder for berries or orange slices, nutmeats, suet, and ground beef. They also like syrup, and some learn to use hummingbird feeders. They're among the birds that appreciate your providing nesting materials such as thread, string, or yarn. Remember to keep the pieces short (six to eight inches) so the birds don't get entangled in loops and strangle themselves.

About half the diet of Baltimore orioles is animal, including gypsy moth larvae, grasshoppers, tent caterpillars, and leaf beetles. The nestlings are fed exclusively on insects, at first regurgitated by the parent birds. Orioles are fond of soft fruits and berries, green peas, mountain ash, and the seeds of garden flowers such as hollyhocks and sunflowers. We know it's time to harvest the pears when the orioles begin spending their time in the tree. Fall migration to the tropics begins in September, though scattered individuals may remain until October.

ORCHARD ORIOLE

Orchard orioles, found in the same range as Baltimore orioles, are sometimes overlooked because their colors are more muted. Novices may even think them the same species. Where the Baltimore oriole is brilliant orange, the orchard oriole is chestnut. His tail is entirely black, he has less white in the wing, and he's slightly smaller. As the name implies, orchard orioles frequently nest in orchards. Their diet, fortunately, is mostly insects, although they sometimes eat mulberries. Their stay is quite brief:

Baltimore oriole

Bullock's oriole

they raise one brood and then they're gone, usually by the end of July. They seldom come to feeders but have sometimes been attracted by bread spread with jelly.

BULLOCK'S ORIOLE

Finally we come to Bullock's oriole, which is larger than either the Baltimore or orchard oriole. The male is similar to the Baltimore oriole in plumage but has orange cheeks and a white wing patch. Some hybridization occurs where the ranges of the two overlap. Their habits are similar. Occasionally Bullock's orioles are blamed for damage to fruit crops, especially cherries and apricots. Their insect eating habits probably balance whatever damage they do.

MEADOWLARKS

Meadowlarks are members of the *Icteridae* family that rarely come to feeders. They can occasionally be attracted to grain scattered on the ground.

MOCKINGBIRDS

The mimic thrushes, *Mimidae*, are related both to true thrushes and wrens, having some characteristics of each. This strictly American family includes mockingbirds, catbirds, and thrashers.

The mockingbird, the most famous of southern birds, has been gradually expanding its range and is now found regularly as far north as Massachusetts. In the east the mockingbird is resident throughout its range, but there is some tendency toward migration in the West. Some shifting towards warmer climates is expected in cold weather. In the northern reaches of their range, mockingbirds are more likely to be found near the coast (or a well-stocked feeder) in the winter.

There is one theory that mockingbirds imitate all those bird songs and make those other remarkable noises by coincidence rather than by mimicry. *Mimidae* have seven pairs of intrinsic syringeal muscles, whereas many other species have only one pair.

mockingbird

They produce sounds more usually made by rusty gates, squeaking tricycles, crickets, dogs, and frogs. Believe what you will; I plan to continue loyal to the mimicry theory.

Mockingbirds were popular as cage birds before the practice of selling wild birds became illegal. Some were captured as nestlings, others bred in captivity. They have a lot going for them in terms of interesting behavior, even apart from their unquestioned vocal abilities. They dance and perform somersaults in mid-air, apparently just for the fun of it. They love to tease dogs and cats, which they often chase or dive-bomb. They harass snakes and drive intruders of whatever species from the vicinity of their nests. They indulge in free-for-alls among themselves or attack their own images reflected in hubcaps or basement windows. A mockingbird is seldom without a project.

Mockingbirds are quite happy to live near man. My friend Carmen used to feed them raisins from the windowsill of her third-floor apartment in the middle of Washington, D. C. They are so fond of raisins that when the price of their favorite delicacy became high, my parents in Florida told me that the retired folk who fed them were quite disturbed. How do you explain inflation to a bird?

Luckily, mockingbirds are adaptable and will eat quite a variety of feeder foods. Such items as American or cottage cheese, apples, berries, currants, nutmeats, peanut butter, suet, doughnuts, bread crumbs, and small grains are quite acceptable. A variety of plants will make your yard appealing to them. They like cabbage palmetto, date palms, euonymus, cotoneaster, blueberries, cherries, asparagus, banana, barberry, American beauty berry, camphor tree, sour gum, sumac, mulberry, yucca, cactus, and persimmons. In addition, they eat flies, beetles, ants, caterpillars, grasshoppers, and boll weevils. Doubtless they can survive without raisins.

CATBIRDS

Catbirds are likely to be found in thickets, especially near water, all over the United States except in parts of the Far West and Southwest. Since they prefer shrubby growth, the settlement of the continent has provided additional habitat for them. Conse-

catbird

quently, their numbers have increased since the seventeenth century. For a time, their fondness for thickets earned them a bad reputation. People believed they were hunting nestlings of other species to destroy. Sometimes they *sound* like cats; they appear to sneak around; therefore, they must be villains. Happily, it has been discovered that they don't engage in such dastardly activities.

Catbirds are friendly and relatively tame, but their liking for tangled shrubbery and their ability as ventriloquists makes them hard to observe. Ours are firmly established in the raspberry patch but will come to the feeders for a variety of foods. They, too, dote on raisins, especially steamed ones, and have a taste for soft berries like raspberries, blackberries, grapes, and elderberries. They'll eat suet, walnut meats, cheese, and bread at feeders, and currants, apples, and oranges as well. In your garden, they'll be attracted to sand cherries, Boston ivy, autumn and cherry elaeagnus, black gum, blueberries, honeysuckle, alder, sumac, and cherries. In the summertime they eat a lot of insects. One source reports that they eat potato bugs, and I wish they'd get to work on mine. Get out of those raspberries, and into the potato patch! They eat ants, Japanese and other beetles, caterpillars, and grasshoppers. They're addicted to bathing.

BROWN THRASHER

The brown thrasher, found only east of the Great Plains, is reddish brown, with a long tail, streaked breast, and long curved bill. He has a reputation for attacking people who venture too near his nest. Although thrashers have as great a fondness for bathing in water as catbirds, they prefer to live in dry thickets. They take dust baths, too.

Like the other members of the *Mimidae* family, thrashers are accomplished vocalists. However, they're less common around human habitation. American beauty bush, black gum, currants, blueberries, raspberries, elderberries, and cherries may lure them to your garden. At the feeder, they'll choose cheese, bread, raisins, cracked corn, and walnut meats—which they'll steal from other birds, if they get the chance. Their natural diet includes insects, particularly beetles and caterpillars. They also feed on grubs, cutworms, grasshoppers, wasps, and wireworms.

The California thrasher is smaller than the brown thrasher and has a sickle-shaped bill. This formidable weapon assists him in his aggressive defense of his nest. He's entirely willing to attack people if they venture too close to his family. California thrashers like sumac, elderberry, pyracantha, privet, grapes, berries, and weed seeds. Their insect food includes ants, wasps, bees, termites, and beetles. At the feeder, they're omnivorous, devouring bread, dog biscuits, suet, raisins, currants, seeds, grains, and berries with a fine lack of discrimination. They try to drive other birds away and are often successful.

brown thrasher

Other western thrashers, some restricted to small ranges within our borders, include the sage thrasher, the long-billed, the curved-billed, Bendire's, Leconte's, Palmer's, and the crissal thrasher. These birds have in common a preference for dry habitat. All of them are noted for vocal agility.

CHICKADEES

A group of us were seated in a large clearing in the woods on a perfect September morning. We were talking and drinking coffee about four feet from a tubular feeder stocked with sunflower seeds. Other feeders on the lawn got sporadic attention, but that tubular one so close to us was the scene of constant activity. Black-capped chickadees chattered at us and each other companionably, clinging to house, feeder, and windowsill, and scolding the cat prowling hopefully among us.

These charming birds are part of the *Paridae* family, a family dear to the hearts of bird lovers. They come to windowsills with

black-capped chickadee

complete confidence and are easily persuaded to eat from the hand. Black-capped chickadees are found all over the northern part of the continent from coast to coast. They're year-round residents throughout most of their range, although the ones you see at your feeder in summer may not be the same individuals as those in winter.

They're woodland birds that will often move into orchards or shade trees. Their natural food is largely insects, even in winter (when they feed on eggs and pupae), but they do eat some seeds, fruits, and berries.

To attract black-capped chickadees to your garden, you need trees. They like balsam firs, locust, birch seeds and buds, butternuts, blueberries, bayberries, and the berries of poison ivy. Their inquisitive and trusting nature often leads them to be among the first visitors to a new feeder. It should come as no surprise, considering the proportion of animal food in their natural diet, that they like suet, but that's not all. I've mentioned their fondness for sunflower seeds. They also eat squash and pumpkin seeds, peanuts or peanut butter, butternuts, oats, bread, and doughnuts. They sometimes develop a liking for honey and syrup.

CAROLINA CHICKADEE

Carolina chickadees are almost identical in appearance to black-capped chickadees, but noticeably smaller. Their ranges overlap only slightly. The Carolina chickadee is native to the Southeast. That the two don't hybridize in the small range common to them is strong evidence that they're separate species despite their striking similarities.

The berries of poison ivy seem to be the Carolina chickadees' favorite vegetable food, but they also like cashews, almonds, sweet gum seeds, acorns, and other seeds. Their chief animal food is moths and caterpillars, but their diet also includes plant lice, spiders, and leaf hoppers. At the feeder, try American and cottage cheese in addition to bread, suet, peanut butter, nutmeats, and sunflower, squash, and pumpkin seeds. They consider a bone that has a bit of meat and gristle still clinging to it an absolute feast.

Similar to these species is the mountain chickadee, a bit larger than the black-capped. You're most apt to find him in coniferous mountain areas from the Rockies west to the Pacific Coast, except in the Pacific Northwest. Like the Carolina and the black-capped chickadees, its food is largely insect, but it also eats berries and seeds. At feeders, mountain chickadees particularly relish pinyon nuts and suet. As friendly and curious as the others, mountain chickadees can become so tamed that they will eat from your hand.

Few of us will have the opportunity to feed the boreal or brown-capped chickadee, which lives in the great north woods. In extremely cold winters, our most northerly areas may have boreal chickadee visitors. Although it is most of all an insect eater, especially aphids, beetles, ants, and wasps, the boreal chickadee consumes pine, balsam fir, and birch seeds and cedar berries. At feeders it likes bread, bacon grease, peanut butter, suet, and sunflower seeds.

TITMICE

You'll hear the *Paridae* family referred to both as the titmouse family and the chickadee family. It also contains bushtits and verdins. All of these birds are prodigious consumers of small insects and their eggs, winter and summer. They eat some seeds and berries too, but in relatively small numbers.

The best known of the titmice is probably the tufted titmouse, resident over much of the United States east from the Plains. He's our only small gray bird with a crest. Although the tufted titmouse was formerly absent north of New Jersey, its range seems to be extending, especially in New York State and southern New England. Particularly in winter, it's common to see titmice in the company of other woodland birds such as woodpeckers, nuthatches, chickadees, and creepers.

Like the chickadees, titmice rely on insect food as their staple item of diet, eating caterpillars, wasps, beetles, and various other insects and their eggs. When planning your garden, you might want to keep in mind that the vegetable food they prefer includes almonds, acorns, cashews, beechnuts, butternuts, mulberries, honeysuckle, wax myrtle berries, and the seeds of locusts. At feeders, titmice eat cantaloupe seeds, bread, nutmeats, peanuts, peanut butter, suet, piecrust, doughnuts, and safflower and sunflower seeds. Like the other acrobatic members of the family, they're happy to use a swinging feeder.

titmouse

Other species of chickadees and titmice are found in very restricted ranges and are not likely to be personally known to many birders. On the western slope of the coastal mountains in Oregon and California, you'll find their tiny relatives, the bushtits, and in high, dry country in the Southwest, the verdin, a diminutive yellow-headed bird.

WARBLER FAMILY

There has been some change in nomenclature in the warbler family, now known as *Parulidae.* For a while they were called *Compsothlypidae,* and before that, *Mniotilidae.* If you're looking for a particular species, especially in older books, use the name warblers first.

The warbler family is large, containing over 150 species. Primarily insectivorous and arboreal, they seldom come to feeders. Especially at migration times, though, you may see them in your yard. Some will be attracted to water; others will visit feeding stations. Because there are so many of them, we'll concentrate mainly on those that are most frequently seen around homes.

ENDANGERED SPECIES

It has been estimated that 40 percent of the world's forests will disappear in the next twenty years and that this loss of habitat will result in destruction of 400,000 to 500,000 species of living things. That's a fifth of the total, a startling number of endangered species. Not all of that total is presently considered endangered, but one of the species is very well known. It has had much attention devoted to it because its needs are incredibly specific. Few of us have ever seen Kirtland's warbler, but we've been made aware of its plight.

In the summertime Kirtland's warblers inhabit six counties in Michigan. They winter in the Bahamas. The population has been steadily declining, but individuals have recently been reported in Quebec. Whether the birds sighted were strays or pioneers expanding their range is not known. Apart from loss of habitat (they like Jack pines, only of a certain size), Kirtland's warblers are badly afflicted by a related problem, parasitism by cowbirds. Cowbirds expand their range, moving in when farmers do, after loggers have removed the pine trees the warblers need.

Kirtland's warblers are not feeder birds, and I call attention to them only because each of the numerous warblers occupies a certain environmental niche. It is often so well adapted to that niche that it's capable of utilizing no other. If the environment changes, therefore, some birds are doomed to suffer and may disappear entirely. Others may become more abundant and yet remain little known to us.

MYRTLE WARBLER

One such warbler is the myrtle warbler, the most abundant of all. It may be identified by its white throat, yellow rump, and

myrtle warbler

yellow patches on the sides of the breast. It breeds in northern coniferous forests and winters from New England to the South, Southwest, and California coast. Primarily an insect eater, it also eats wax myrtle berries, euonymus, almonds, butternuts, red cedar and poison ivy berries, and sumac and goldenrod seeds. At feeders it consumes bread, doughnuts, cornmeal, peanut butter, nutmeats, sunflower seeds, and suet.

Rather similar in appearance, except for a yellow throat, is the Audubon warbler, found west of the Great Plains. A bird lover in South Dakota had one stray which spent the winter at her feeder. She made piecrust for it.

OTHER WARBLERS

The orange-crowned warbler breeds in the West and Northwest but winters in the South and has been found as far north as Massachusetts. It will occasionally visit feeders for bread, suet, and nutmeats. The black and white warbler is found from the Great Plains east and occasionally visits feeders for suet. The pine warbler's range is similar, and it often comes to feeders. Its favorite delicacies are bread, piecrust, cornmeal, peanut butter, nutmeats, and suet.

The yellow-breasted chat, or wood warbler, is the largest warbler (about 7½ inches) and is regarded as eccentric, clownish, and altogether unwarbler-like. It may be attracted by blackberries, blueberries, elderberries, dogwood, and sumac. It's found all over the contiguous states. So is the yellow warbler, that bird which has been known to erect six-story nests in order to cover up cowbird eggs. Unfortunately, yellow warblers don't seem to be able to distinguish their own nestlings. If the cowbird egg happens to hatch, the tiny foster parents rear it.

Among the warblers you may see is the American redstart, unmistakable with its orange patches in wings and tail. It is likely to come to a birdbath. In the Northeast, it may be joined by the Blackburnian warbler.

The warblers are often compared to butterflies because of their flitting habits and small size. You're most likely to see them in your garden during migration. There are tremendous numbers of warblers, and their habitual activities make precise observations arduous and often frustrating. Bird lovers who do most of their watching from the kitchen window will not have much chance to become familiar with warblers except those few, such as the myrtle warbler, which readily accept feeders.

American redstart

HOUSE SPARROW

When is a sparrow not a sparrow? When it's a weaver finch. The family of weaver finches, *Ploceidae*, contains the house sparrow, or English sparrow. One of the commonly despised birds, the house sparrow, like starlings and rock doves (the common pigeon of urban areas), is an immigrant. The first house sparrows were introduced to this continent during the 1850s and they proved extraordinarily adaptable and prolific. They were brought from the Old World, where they had long been accustomed to city life. Our native birds had not yet adapted to urban conditions when the house sparrows arrived and usurped the place that one or more native species might eventually have taken as their own.

house sparrow

They multiplied and multiplied, producing two or three (some birders swear they sometimes produced as many as five) broods a year. It is thought that the coming of motor vehicles helped to stabilize their numbers because the gradual disappearance of horses from our streets meant a loss of food to the birds. They fed not only on grain spills but on the waste grain in manure as well. At the peak of their population explosion, it's estimated that they were not only the most abundant bird in their North American range but that their numbers in some areas were *double* those of all other birds together. Diseases as well as weather and predators eventually took their toll, but many believe that the largest single limiting factor was the proliferation of motor vehicles.

BAD REPUTATION

House sparrows are not now the problem they once were, but they still get criticism. A native bird might be described as resourceful or careless in habit; a house sparrow is cunning and filthy. But despite their bad reputation, despite the observable fact that they moved into our cities and kept any similar native species from doing that instead, despite their adaptability, they have not seriously challenged native birds except where *people* have altered the environment too radically for the original inhabitants.

There's no need to encourage house sparrows to come to feeding stations. They're opportunists, and they'll be among the first to discover the existence of a new source of food. But there is no need to poison, trap, or shoot them. They do very little harm that isn't balanced by some of their more acceptable habits. Yes, they're fond of grain and may help themselves where cereals are grown. They may feed on newly sprouted garden vegetables. They're also fond, however, of the seeds of crabgrass, dandelion, and ragweed. Sudden infestations of insects—Japanese beetles, for example—will attract them, even though normally their diet doesn't include a large amount of animal matter.

House sparrows may nest in places you don't want them. The ivy climbing up your chimney is a favorite spot, and they'll use it for warmth and protection in winter as readily as for a nesting site during the breeding period. We've noted some of the precautions that can be taken to prevent their occupying bluebird houses or other nesting boxes you've provided. They'll steal from other birds at the feeder, but they prefer ground feeding or stable feeders. A hanging feeder will discourage them from gobbling up all the bread, seeds, and suet you set out.

The house sparrow's only near relative in this country is the European tree sparrow, another introduced species, this one from Germany. It was released near St. Louis in 1870 and is still found only in that area. It is a bit smaller than the house sparrow and somewhat less aggressive. They're similar in appearance except that the European tree sparrow's crown is chocolate rather than black, and it has a black ear spot as well as a smaller black throat spot.

NUTHATCHES

That avian acrobat, the nuthatch, is one of our common feeder birds. Its family, the *Sittidae*, has thin bills, sturdy bodies, short squared tails, and strong feet and legs. They're distinctive in appearance but even more so in behavior. They consistently go

nuthatch

down tree trunks head-first. All of the nuthatches will use swinging feeders.

The white-breasted nuthatch is resident over most of the country throughout the year. About half its diet is animal, consisting of ants, beetles, flies, locusts, spiders, and scale insects as well as insect eggs. The plant part includes beechnuts, acorns, and hickory nuts, pine, fir, and maple seeds, mountain ash and juniper berries, apples, and sunflower seeds. Nuthatches store food. They're very fond of suet but also visit feeders for bread and doughnuts and the seeds of sunflower, squash, and pumpkin. They'll nibble on raw beef and carrots if you'll supply them. White-breasted nuthatches are often found in the company of kinglets, downy woodpeckers, chickadees, and creepers. Ours are so tame they merely move to the other side of the feeder and peer at us from underneath if we go out to fill it while they're dining.

RED-BREASTED NUTHATCH

The red-breasted nuthatch is found in the same range, but its numbers seem to fluctuate greatly. It has been postulated that this is a result of fluctuations in its favorite foods. The seeds of spruce, fir, and maple are preferred. In times of heavy snow cover especially, it feeds on the seeds of weeds such as ragweed and dock. It drinks sap from the holes left by sapsuckers. A tame creature, it comes to suet, sunflower seeds, and nutmeats at feeders. It can be trained to take them from the hand. Like the white-breasted nuthatch, it carries food away from feeders to hide it.

BROWN-HEADED NUTHATCH

The brown-headed nuthatch is found most often in pine woods in the Southern states. It is especially fond of pine seeds, but it also eats nuts, ants, scale insects, and insect eggs. It comes to feeders for suet, bread, nutmeats, and sunflower seeds. The pygmy nuthatch is actually the same size as the brown-headed, and there is some suspicion that it is a subspecies. It's found only from southwestern South Dakota westward. It too prefers coniferous trees as a habitat.

STARLINGS

Another immigrant, the starling had a later start than the house sparrow and was successfully introduced at only one place, Central Park in New York City, in 1890. It is now found from coast to coast, in abundance, and has achieved the dubious distinction of displacing the house sparrow from first place as the bird people best like to despise.

Starlings are members of the Old World family *Sturnidae*, which includes also the talking mynah bird. They're capable mimics, though not as competent in that respect as our native mimic thrushes. They can, when they choose, sing melodiously. They don't, in practice, choose that course very often, seeming to delight in hoarse squawks and shrill squeals.

Mankind's quarrel with starlings quickens in proportion to their numbers. Since the species is adaptable, intelligent, and prolific, the battle is growing, especially in cities. Their characteristic gathering into huge flocks is one of the major causes of our dismay. Much as a city dweller might admire their spectacular aerial maneuvers, when thousands of them roost on a bridge or a building they pose a problem. Similarly, when enormous flocks descend on an orchard or grain field, their very numbers assure a great amount of damage in a short time. Those whose crops disappear are unlikely to think kindly of the marauders even if reminded that starlings launch similar attacks on insect pests, especially when there is a virulent infestation.

The starling has been described as "casually omnivorous." Beetles, fruits, berries, nuts, seeds, meat, suet, bread, carrion—you name it, a starling will eat it. The son of friends in New Jersey swears that they steal sneakers for the sheer joy of ingesting them. I think he exaggerates. They're usually on any list you see of feeder pests, charged with tearing suet bags in their greediness and chasing more desirable birds from the feeder.

starling

Unless you live in a city plagued with starlings, you can cope with them without resorting to the practices advocated by some "bird lovers." Some recommend shooting, a difficult method, since it's estimated that starlings can fly fifty miles an hour. You needn't resort to a reign of terror. Starlings will be among the first to discover a new feeding station, but they aren't attracted to swinging feeders, which will discourage competition with some of the smaller birds you especially like. And try to keep an open mind. In the spring, a starling's diet is as high as 90 percent animal. That's insects. Unless you're the operator of a feedlot (one in Caldwell, Idaho, reports that their resident starling flock devours fifteen to twenty tons of potatoes *a day*), a harassed orchardist, or an equally harassed city dweller, you can probably learn to live with starlings.

The nesting behavior of starlings is apt to cause some problems. They prefer to be cavity nesters and may decide to take over all your birdhouses if you don't take great care about the size of the entrance holes. What may be more annoying to you personally is their fondness for taking up residence in the ivy growing up your house. A chimney area will claim their interest in winter. Their non-melodious lays may drive you frantic.

The noted authority Forbush talks at some length about the beauty of the starling. I'm prepared to go to some lengths to defend starlings in a general sort of way, but not on aesthetic grounds. We needn't worry about their appearance, though. That's probably the least of their problems. But do try to keep an open mind. If we banish all the troublemakers—the jays and starlings and grackles—we'll have a more peaceful feeder, but a far less interesting one.

OLD WORLD WARBLERS

The family *Sylviidae* is known more familiarly as Old World Warblers. In North America it isn't extensive. It's represented by kinglets and gnatcatchers. The gnatcatchers we'll just mention in passing, since they don't come to feeders.

The golden-crowned kinglet, found on both sides of the Great Plains, is easily identified by its black-bordered orange or yellow cap. In size it ranges from 3½ to four inches. Only the humming-bird is smaller. These migratory birds eat insects and insect eggs almost exclusively but will occasionally take suet at a feeder. They nest in coniferous forests but may be seen in winter in deciduous trees and evergreens in the suburbs. They have the reputation of being tame, active little birds. In winter they're likely to be seen with chickadees, brown creepers, and downy woodpeckers.

golden-crowned warblers

Only the male of the ruby-crowned kinglets has a red patch, and it isn't often visible. If you see what seems to be a kinglet and don't notice color on the head, it's a ruby-crowned kinglet. It has white eye-rings and is nearly as tiny as the golden-crowned king-let. What everyone seems to notice about ruby-crowned kinglets is their songs, which are cheerful and remarkably loud. These hardy little birds seem quite undamaged by winter storms. They eat in-sects for about nine-tenths of their diet, but also consume some seeds and berries. At feeders they regularly eat nutmeats, peanuts, and suet. If syrup is available, they'll sample that.

Ruby-crowned kinglets, though very active, are tame. During migrations they'll often be found in the company of wood warblers, bluebirds, and nuthatches, but ordinarily they're not as gregarious as the golden-crowned kinglets. Despite the great differences in size, the family is closely related to the thrushes. The young birds, however, are not spotted, as juvenile thrushes always are.

THRUSHES

The thrushes, whose family name is *Turdidae*, are reknowned for singing (the European nightingale is a thrush). Thrushes are numerous and found all over the world except in parts of Polynesia. Although they are not regularly visitors at most feeding stations, one or more species is likely to be a resident of or a frequent visitor to your garden. They are included here for that reason.

ROBIN

The robin, recognized by even the smallest child, is our largest thrush, measuring ten inches. He's found all over the continent throughout spring and summer. Robins migrate by day, and often they don't go far, though some reach southern Mexico. We think of them as relatively tame, but they're not ordinarily feeder birds in the north. If they come to a feeder, they're likely to sample bread, ground toast, raisins, and fruits. Occasionally a robin decides to terrorize feeder society, but it's a passing phenomenon. It's much more likely that your robins will be attracted to the garden for their animal and vegetable food—and to your birdbath. Robins are unabashedly fond of bathing.

Robins eat earthworms, but they eat a lot of other things, too. Ask anyone who has a strawberry patch or a cherry tree. To protect the fruits you want for your own use, provide a substitute, an attractive substitute such as the mulberry. Three other favorites that are especially attractive to robins are pyracantha, mountain ash, and chinatree berries. Robins tend to like fruit over-ripe, whereupon they proceed to get themselves thoroughly drunk,

robin

even falling to the ground in a stupor. It seems hardly the way for
a bird to preserve its health, to say nothing of its dignity.

Among robins' other food favorites are the berries of Japanese
and American barberry, honeysuckle, juniper, and Russian olives.
They'll go after grapes and the fruits of cotoneaster, Virginia
creeper, black gum, currant, date palm, persimmon, American
beauty berry, bittersweet, euonymus, madrone, cranberries, cabbage palmetto, camphor tree, pepper tree, and chokecherries. Provide plenty of alternatives and you'll have less competition for
your own favorites. Besides earthworms, robins eat flies, caterpillars, spiders, grasshoppers, ants, weevils, and tiny fish, to mention
some of their animal food.

Robins are fond of nesting close to human habitation. They
raise two or three broods a year. Because of their proximity to
houses, young robins sometimes fall victim to cats. No less an authority than the Audubon Society itself has pointed out, however,
that their population remains stable because there are virtually no
wild predators in such environs. The robin is another species that
has become more plentiful and has extended its range, especially
in the South and West, because of increasing human use of the
continent. Its natural habitat is barrens, open woods, or the edges
of forests. It has proved capable of adapting to suburban life. At
one time, oddly enough, it was considered a game bird and was
shot by the thousands.

Robins are apt to be seen on lawns and in gardens at close
range, so you may have a chance some time to observe their anting behavior. They are also among the birds that won't tolerate a

cowbird egg in the nest, but will chuck it out immediately. A robin sometimes uses the same nest, after refurbishing it, for successive broods. It also uses old nests of other species. Occasionally it builds a new nest on top of an old one. Structures six nests high have been reported. Albino birds sometimes occur among thrushes, including robins. I've seen photographs but never the genuine article; however, my bird-loving aunt in Illinois saw one in her shrubbery and snapped its picture. She reports that the other robins kept their distance.

Many robins can be found in the North in winter. Apparently they forsake lawns during that season and move into marshy or swampy places.

BLUEBIRDS

Robins are easily identified because of their colorful plumage. Even more colorful are their much smaller cousins, the bluebirds. There are three major species, all of them very attractive: the eastern, the western, and the mountain bluebird. Their habits and diets are quite similar. In the summertime their food consists mainly of insects; later they add some fruits.

Bluebirds can be attracted to stationary feeders. Special enclosed ones that exclude larger birds are available commercially. Their preferred feeder foods are raisins and fruits, but they'll also sample bread, peanuts, and peanut butter. Among the insects

bluebird

bluebirds normally eat are grasshoppers, beetles, caterpillars, and crickets, but not many flying insects. In addition to poison ivy and sumac berries, they'll eat blackberries, blueberries, currants, and the berries of asparagus, dogwood, chokecherry, and huckleberry, to say nothing of elaeagnus, date palms, cotoneaster, Virginia creeper, euonymus, mountain ash, bittersweet, black gum, and camphor tree.

The western bluebird is similar in appearance to the eastern except that its throat also is blue, and the red of the breast extends to the shoulders and back. An eater of terrestrial insects when they're available, it switches to fruits, berries, and weed seeds in winter.

The mountain bluebird, which occurs in a wide range from the Great Plains west, has a blue back, paler blue breast, and a white belly. The northern part of its range appears to be expanding eastward. Its food habits are similar to those of the other bluebirds, largely insectivorous in summer and turning more to fruits in the winter.

Bluebirds early captured the affection of men through their beauty and melodious songs and because their habits are largely beneficial to us. They're relatively tame and accept the nesting boxes provided for them. Periodically, they have suffered large population losses because of severe weather in either their winter range or breeding range, to which they return fairly early. These losses usually provoke a rush of birdhouse building on man's part. It's important to give bluebirds this help to maintain their numbers because of the competition for nesting sites from starlings and house sparrows.

MORE THRUSHES

Townsend's solitaire had been described as looking like a smallish, rather dull mockingbird. It's a bird of rough, mountainous country, found from the Black Hills west. Its song is highly regarded. Flying insects provide the bulk of the solitaire's diet. Although it doesn't regularly come to feeders, it can be enticed to your yard by juniper, cedar, and other plants that have berries in winter.

The other thrushes, handsome in a more muted way, are not so likely to be recognized by the novice birder. The wood thrush, slightly smaller than the robin, has a reddish brown head and a creamy breast with brown spots. At various times it has been called the wood robin, song thrush, and swamp robin. Though its natural habitat is deep woods, it is frequently found near human habitation from the Great Plains east. It winters in southern Mexico to Panama. If lured to a feeder, the wood thrush will eat suet, peanut butter, raisins, bread products, and cornmeal. Some people have fed it honey or syrup. More than half its food is insect: ants, beetles, spiders, grasshoppers. Like a few other birds, it's said to eat the Colorado potato beetle. The wood thrush likes elderberries, mulberries, strawberries, chokecherries, and the fruits of the dogwood and sumac. When it nests near people, its favorite sites are beech trees, grape arbors, dogwoods, and rhododendrons, usually three to twelve feet above the ground.

HERMIT THRUSH

The hermit thrush, as its name might suggest, is likely to be found alone. He's also known as the American nightingale and the swamp angel. Those names indicate clearly his vocal abilities. The earliest thrush to arrive in spring, he's also the last to leave in the fall, and a few winter in the North. The hermit thrush is smaller than the wood thrush and has a reddish brown tail which contrasts with its dull brown back. At the feeder, he'll be tempted by nutmeats and suet. His natural food is spiders, ants, crickets, wasps, caterpillars, and beetles as well as wild fruits and berries. To attract him to your yard, try euonymus, bittersweet, privet, barberry, mountain ash, black gum, and Virginia creeper. Hermit thrushes also like the fruits of wild grape, sumac, and poison ivy. They're unlikely to raid domestic berry patches, seeming to prefer the wild berries. Their preferred nesting sites are on the ground in woods, preferably near a bog or creek, where they raise one to three broods a year. They are sometimes parasitized by cowbirds.

None of the other thrushes is likely to come to feeders, but olive-backed thrushes may be attracted to sand cherries in your garden, especially during migration.

TANAGERS

The family *Thraupidae* (formerly *Tangaridae*) contains singularly colorful birds. The western tanager, yellow with black wings and a red head, is normally found from the Black Hills to the Pacific, but some individuals are found in the East nearly every year during migration. They spend the winter in Central America.

Their food is insects, fruit, and berries. Western tanagers come regularly to feeders in their range, where they will sample just about anything. In the garden, they like the fruits of mountain ash and, especially, cherries. Their fondness for cherries sometimes gets them into trouble with orchardists, but their appetite for insects perhaps compensates for that problem. The bird lover is likely to be willing to protect his cherries with netting and try to encourage this lovely bird to use his feeder.

SUMMER TANAGER

The summer tanager, at home in the South, is rosy red and, unlike the cardinal, has no crest. It will readily visit feeders for white bread, soft fruits such as banana, suet, and peanut butter. Its appetite for bees has earned it the nickname of bee bird in some places. In addition to bees, its insect food includes wasps, cicadas, flies, weevils, and spiders. Your garden, if it contains blackberries, mulberries, or figs, may be attractive to the "summer redbird."

scarlet tanager

SCARLET TANAGER

The scarlet tanager, a resident of deciduous woods, is easily identified by his black wings and tail. You may see him in your garden, catching insects on the wing, if you live from the Great Plains east to the Atlantic. Unfortunately, he's quite unlikely to appear at your feeder. His food is nine-tenths insects, especially bees and wasps. However, scarlet tanagers (sometimes called black-winged redbirds, or firebirds) eat a few berries too. They seem to like those of the euonymus.

WRENS

Some species of wrens, all insect eaters of the family *Troglodytidae*, are quite common around human habitation. We are unlikely to attract any but the Carolina wren to a feeder, however. Carolina wrens are found as far north as Nebraska and Massachusetts, south to Florida and the Gulf Coast. They'll accept bread crumbs, peanuts, nutmeats, suet, peanut butter, ground meat, and cottage cheese. In the garden, they occasionally snack from bayberries and sweet gum trees. What they really prefer, however, are the insects that constitute about 95 percent of their diet: caterpillars, moths, beetles, grasshoppers, crickets, ants, bees, weevils, and flies.

Providing birdhouses can attract wrens to your property wherever you live. The house wren occurs nearly everywhere in the contiguous United States. Bewick's wren, which resembles the house wren except that it has an unusually long tail, is found in a wide area, excluding Florida, the East Coast, and the Northern Rockies and Plains States. It is apparently expanding its range northward. Despite having overlapping ranges, the two are unlikely to be found together.

wren

The rock wren and canyon wren are confined to the West. The cheerful songs and the feeding habits of the wrens make them welcome to our gardens whether they deign to visit feeders or not.

That does it for the perching birds, the most numerous order both absolutely and at the feeder. We have other popular visitors to consider, but though many of them feed in perfect harmony with the perching birds and some even form loose flocks with them, they are quite different in important respects.

9
A Variety
of
Orders

Though the majority of birds at the feeder will be the perching birds, the order *Passeriformes*, there's no trick to attracting woodpeckers. They belong to the order *Piciformes*, family *Picidae*. Despite great differences in appearance, all woodpeckers have certain physical characteristics in common. You would expect them to have heavy, chisel-like bills to extract the grubs and larvae of insects found under the bark of trees. Their hammering on the wood to get to these delicacies necessitates a strong skull. And, the better to ingest their food once it's uncovered, the woodpeckers have long, extensible tongues. Their legs and feet are sturdy, and most of the family have two toes pointing forward and two pointing backward. Their stiff tail feathers act as a prop to hold them in an appropriate position as they hammer away at the trees.

The speed and skill with which woodpeckers can make holes in trees—or telephone poles or houses, for that matter—have often caused them to be viewed with a certain amount of alarm. When we built a house some years ago in a wooded area, we stumbled into a running feud with a hairy woodpecker which seemed intent on destroying the gable on the eastern side of it. I spent considerable time rushing outdoors to yell at him. There *can't* have been any insects under those shingles, so we surmised that we had removed some of his favorite feeding sites and he couldn't break himself of the location habit. Whether the suet we supplied helped convince him to stop devastating the house is a moot point. Orchardists have often been dismayed by the holes excavated by woodpeckers, but the fact is that the holes are less likely to damage the trees than the woodboring creatures that the woodpeckers search out. If other insects later take up residence in the cavities, woodpeckers are quite ready to dine on them in their turn.

Members of the woodpecker family are largely arboreal (living in trees), with the prominent exception of the flicker. Many of them are resident year-round in their ranges, although they may wander considerably after the breeding season is over. They are cavity nesters, using the chips of wood they remove as nesting material. Some will nest in a birdhouse you provide, especially if it's covered with bark. They definitely prefer a rustic decor. Put a layer of wood chips or shavings on the floor to serve as nesting material. Both sexes incubate the eggs, which are white. Nestlings remain in the nest for a longer time than terrestrial birds do and

downy woodpecker

are well enough developed to fly immediately after quitting the nest. Many woodpeckers roost in their nesting sites.

DOWNY WOODPECKER

Probably the most familiar of the woodpeckers is the downy woodpecker, a favorite at most feeders. This sparrow-sized black and white bird is found all over the United States except in southern Texas and the extreme Southwest. His preferred feeder food is suet. The downy is friendly and tame, found often near man. City parks, open woods, farmyards, or dooryards are equally appealing to him. About three-fourths of his natural food is insects such as beetles, caterpillars, woodboring ants, larvae, and eggs. He rounds out his diet with seeds, berries and fruit, some sap, and the cambium layer of bark. In winter, downy woodpeckers are frequently found in loose flocks with nuthatches and chickadees.

HAIRY WOODPECKER

Hairy woodpeckers closely resemble the downies, but the hairy woodpecker is robin-sized and has a much stouter, heavier bill than does the downy. He's also considerably less common. Though he's found in the same range—in fact, all over the country, including southern Texas and the Southwest—he's less likely to make his home close to man's. During the breeding season, hairy woodpeckers prefer the deep woods. They rear only one brood a year, and the male frequently makes himself a bedroom in a tree adjacent to the nesting site. The nestlings stay in the nest about three weeks (longer than downies) and, like other woodpecker young, are remarkably unlovely. But then, many birds are homely when hatched, and most of them go through one stage or another of looking at least awkward, gawky, or dishevelled.

Hairy woodpeckers are most likely to come to feeders during the winter and will appreciate meatbones in addition to suet. Their major food is woodboring beetles, but they also like beechnuts, hazelnuts, acorns, pine seeds, and pinyons. They are less often seen with chickadees and other smaller birds than are the downies; but then, they're less often seen at all.

FLICKERS

Heigh-ho. Yarrup. Clape. Hairy wicket. Yellow hammer. That's just a sampling of the 125 names by which the flicker has been known. And there's no question that the flicker is known, all over the continent. For one thing, flickers are big—about thirteen inches (robins measure ten inches, blue jays twelve inches). They're noisy, too. The yellow-shafted flicker is found east of the Rockies; the red-shafted flicker is found from the eastern foothills of the Rockies to the Pacific. The red and the yellow are listed as two different species, but ornithologists have begun to think maybe they are actually subspecies. The two interbreed wherever their ranges overlap, and their observable differences are in plumage only.

Flickers are present throughout much of their range during the entire year, but tend to shift their populations southward for the winter. They nest in tree cavities or telephone poles, but they're willing to use man-made boxes too, preferably with entrance holes three inches in diameter and facing south. They raise one or two broods a year, and the nestlings remain in the cavity as long as twenty-eight days. Like other woodpeckers, the nestlings make a hissing noise if disturbed. Some observers think it sounds like a swarm of bees.

You'll find flickers as frequently as downy woodpeckers around the lawn and garden, but you'll find them also in the woods or on the edges of swamps, in brushlands or open country. Unlike most other woodpeckers, they hunt some of their food on the ground. Over half of their diet is insects, especially ants. They eat more ants than any other bird known. But they'll chomp also on beetles, wasps, crickets, grasshoppers, and caterpillars. Every once in a while they even catch insects on the wing. Flickers eat a wide variety of plant material. They like plums, raspberries, blackberries, and chokecherries, poison ivy berries and sumac, dogwood, magnolias, oak, and mountain ash, euonymus, black gum, beech, Virginia creeper—you name it, flickers will sample the fruit or nuts. They snack on suet and peanut butter at the feeder.

red-bellied woodpecker

RED-BELLIED WOOD-PECKER

The red-bellied woodpecker is also called the zebra wood-pecker, the chad, and the ram-shack. Although often thought of as a representative southern bird, it's found all over the United States east of the Plains, except in the northeastern portion. It doesn't actually migrate, but it shifts southward after the breeding season and does a little wandering in the fall. Only a third of its diet is insects: ants, beetles, grasshoppers, and caterpillars. Its vegetable food includes cashews, beechnuts, almonds, butternuts, acorns, and various seeds and fruit, especially oranges. At the feeder, pieces of orange are particularly well received, but bread, suet, peanut butter, nutmeats, and cracked corn are accepted too.

RED-HEADED WOODPECKER

The red-headed woodpecker is found in most of the same area as the red-bellied woodpecker, but also ranges up into the Northeast. Its food choices are similar to those of the red-bellied woodpecker, and it exhibits the same tendency to store acorns and nuts in crevices for later use. Friends in Florida had a red-headed woodpecker visit their feeder regularly for sunflower seeds, which he carried to the eaves and dropped down a pipe supporting their ham radio antenna.

The red-headed woodpecker likes beechnuts, acorns, and cherries, chokecherries, other fruits and berries, and grain. It eats insects for about a third of its diet, sometimes catching flies on the wing. Bread, peanut butter, corn, nutmeats, and suet attract this noisy, robin-sized bird to the feeder.

PILEATED WOODPECKER

An extremely eye-catching woodpecker, which occasionally visits feeders for nutmeats and suet, is the pileated woodpecker. He's the size of a crow and has a bright red crest. Although pileated woodpeckers are habitually birds of the deep woods, they seem to be adapting to man's presence and now are found even in wooded suburbs. They're rather quiet birds, but can be startling, to say the least. I saw my first one from horseback; when he flew by, both horse and I jumped about three feet.

Pileated woodpeckers are known by some interesting names, including logcock, Wood Kate, and (a series I can only assume resulted from first impressions) Great God woodpecker, Good God woodpecker, and Lord God woodpecker. They usually nest in dead trees or tall stumps, in which they dig prodigious cavities. Their insect food includes carpenter ants and beetles in all stages of development. Seeking these creatures in tree trunks, they excavate holes four to eight inches deep and rectangular in shape. They also eat wild fruits, berries, and nuts.

Sometimes birders mistake pileated woodpeckers for the extremely rare ivory-billed woodpecker (which is larger: twenty inches to the seventeen inches of the pileated). Not only is its ivory bill distinctive, but the lower halves of its wings, when folded, are white. The pileated woodpecker's wings are black. In addition to being rare, the ivory-billed woodpecker can be found only in the forests of the South Atlantic and Gulf states.

YELLOW-BELLIED SAPSUCKER

On the other hand, the yellow-bellied sapsucker, between sparrows and robins in size, is found over most of the country. Besides sap and insects, it eats fruits and berries. At the feeder it is more likely to accept apple bits, cherries, or strawberries than anything else except an occasional sample of suet or nutmeats.

The tongue of the sapsucker is brush-like and therefore not adapted to gathering the kinds of insects that many woodpeckers eat. It's perfect for its purpose, though. The bird sometimes gets quite boisterous from imbibing fermented sap, especially in spring. Margaret Millar, in *The Birds and the Beasts Were There*, tells a wonderful story of an inebriated sapsucker vigorously defending his source against a hopeful oriole.

MEXICAN WOODPECKER

The ladder-backed, or Mexican, woodpecker is familiar to bird lovers of the Southwest. This smallish, red-crowned fellow can be found in deserts, canyons, and brushy areas, where he feeds on woodboring beetles and the fruits of wild plants, including cactus. He also frequents urban areas and may be tempted by suet fastened to a tree.

Lewis' woodpecker, a mountain species, is usually encountered from the Rockies westward, though he does visit the Plains sometimes. He too may be discovered in towns and suburbs. He has a distinct fondness for fruits in addition to acorns and insects, and is one of the multitude of birds attracted by cherries. His nickname, "crow woodpecker," refers to his habit of flight, not to his size. He's just a bit larger than the hairy woodpecker.

That doesn't cover, by any means, all of the woodpeckers. They're a fascinating lot, but to see some of them you'll probably have to take to the woods. Some have restricted ranges; some are rather reclusive. We must go on to birds more likely to take advantage of your feeding station.

PIGEONS AND DOVES

Such are pigeons and doves, the order *Columbiformes*, the family *Columbidae*. The first thing we ought to do is clear up the sticky business of the difference between pigeons and doves. Simple. There is none. The terms may be (and are) used interchangeably. You'll perhaps hear people insisting that pigeons are bigger than doves. Maybe so, generally; but in England the largest species is called the ring dove. So much for fine distinctions.

Then there's the popular misconception that doves are gentle, symbols of peace and love. Don't you believe it. Tender to their

ringed turtle dove

mates (though occasionally inconstant), protective of their offspring, yes. But two males meeting when the breeding season gets
under way means a horrendous fracas. Wild or feral losers usually
fly away unharmed; domestic or captive ones are often seriously
(or fatally) injured. And notice too, if you will, their behavior
under the feeder or wherever you scatter food. The dominant ones
relentlessly chase others—of their own or any other ground-
feeding species—away from choice morsels. Those soft, cooing
noises have misled us all.

Now for the wonderful peculiarities of pigeons and doves. Unlike other birds, they don't need to raise their heads to drink.
They submerge their beaks up to the nostrils and sort of inhale.
Normally, they drink mornings and evenings, and since they're
strong, swift flyers, they may go rather long distances for water.
They eat mostly grains, seeds, and fruit. They seem to require
considerable salt and often can be seen scavenging for both salt
and gravel (for their crops) along roadsides.

Doves are careless nest builders, whether they choose a man-
made structure, a tree, or the ground for the nesting site. Egg casualties, from accidents to their flimsy constructions, are commonplace. Both parents share the incubating chores and the care of the
young. Both also produce the secretion known as pigeon milk

which feeds the nestlings early in life. Since neither sex shows any interest in housekeeping tasks, the nest and its environs are definitely untidy—one might say filthy—by the time the squabs are ready to leave home.

Pigeons and doves are found all over the world, in tropical and temperate climates, and object not in the least to encroaching civilization. The passenger pigeon, it is true, is extinct, though it was once probably our most numerous native species. Its extinction is a reprehensible example of squandering a resource, of molesting a species that seemed inexhaustible. The young birds were not only easier to take but commanded a higher price at the market than older ones. Their slaughter and the accompanying disturbance to flocks, combined with the usual run of natural catastrophes, had disastrous consequences.

ROCK DOVE

What we have now, in tremendous numbers, is the rock dove, the commonplace pigeon of urban areas. Like starlings and house sparrows, it was introduced from Europe. It is abundant in wild, feral, and domestic conditions. The wild variety is distinctive, but the feral and domestic birds come in all sorts of color combinations. You're familiar with rock doves; you know one when you see it, whatever the markings may be. Their diet consists entirely of plant food. They'll eat bread, grains of all kinds, and peanuts.

RINGED TURTLE DOVE

Other doves have been introduced and become established in more limited ranges. The ringed turtle dove, a lovely pale bird with dark primaries, is found in Los Angeles. The spotted dove is quite similar in appearance to our native mourning dove but is a little larger. It's easily identified by its collar of black and white spots and its rounded tail with large amounts of white at the corners. After its release near Los Angeles around 1918 it became established there and spread to adjacent areas. It has more recently been released in Florida and Hawaii. At feeders, spotted doves prefer small seeds and cracked corn. A friend in the Los Angeles area observed one in his yard gorging on cat kibbles.

MOURNING DOVE

The mourning dove, found from southern Canada to Mexico, was formerly known as the Carolina or turtle dove. Its numbers in the North have been increasing steadily. The settlement of the continent has provided a favorable habitat for the mourning dove, and it has become more abundant throughout its range. In some areas it is classified as a songbird and is, therefore, protected; in others it is considered a game bird.

We don't bother scattering food for the mourning doves which pay regular calls to our feeders. Most of our friends and neighbors who maintain feeding stations rely on spills to satisfy the ground feeders, and that seems to work. Mourning doves are said to be especially fond of hemp and millet seeds. We see them daily in pastures and mowings, eating weed seeds. They also partake of beechnuts, small acorns, and grain. Most of the grain they eat is from the ground, so they aren't normally considered a menace to agriculture.

GROUND DOVE

The ground dove, a bird of the southern United States, is much smaller than those so far mentioned, only the size of a sparrow. It's mostly gray, with stubby black tail and chestnut wing linings. Expect it to come to feeders for small grains, cracked corn, or scratch feed and small seeds. It regularly visits lawns, gardens, and farms, but is considered shy. The ground dove eats a few insects, but most of its diet consists of weed seeds, waste grains, and berries.

The Inca dove, just a bit larger, has a long, white-edged tail. It's found in the Southwest, in open lands, parks, farms, lawns, and gardens. It often forages for grain with domestic chickens and other livestock. It also eats weed seeds. The white-winged dove, another resident of the Southwest, is similar to the mourning dove. In some areas it's a game bird. It eats grains and at the feeder is attracted to scratch feed.

The other pigeons and doves resident or occasionally seen on the continent are found in limited ranges or aren't considered feeder birds. The band-tailed pigeon, for example, is primarily a game bird.

HUMMINGBIRDS

From large birds found all over the world we go to a family of small birds found only in North, Central, and South America: the hummingbirds. They're in the order *Apodiformes*, which also includes swifts. The hummingbird family name is *Trochilidae*. There are over 300 species of hummingbirds, ranging in size from 2¼ inches to 8½ inches. Only seventeen species enter the United States, and neither the largest (a native of the Andes) nor the smallest (a resident of Cuba) is among them. Even seventeen strikes me as an embarrassment of riches, since I live in an area that boasts only one: the ruby-throated hummingbird.

hummingbird

As a family, hummingbirds are remarkable, no two ways about it. For one thing, they're tiny. That Cuban hummer is the smallest bird in the world. Our smallest, the calliope, is under three inches, and our largest barely makes five inches. Most of them measure between three and four inches.

Size isn't their only claim on our attention. Take the matter of wings. Most birds have powered downstrokes. In hummingbirds both upstroke and downstroke are powered. They can fly backwards, forwards, and sideways, or, like a helicopter, they can hover. The name, hummingbird, derives from the sound of their wings. They have the fastest wingbeat of all the birds. And they have the most rapid heartbeat. To maintain themselves during the daytime, they need to eat every ten to fifteen minutes. They have the highest relative food consumption of any bird known. They fall into a torpor resembling hibernation, a condition requiring only a twentieth of their normal daytime energy output, at night. Their body temperature drops almost to that of the air. Next morning they arouse almost instantaneously.

Hummingbirds can perch, but they have such weak feet and legs that they can scarcely walk. Their plumage is typically brilliant, iridescent. Their beaks are very long and needle-like. Their tongues are long, double tubed, and sticky, enabling them to cope with sap, nectar, small insects, and hummingbird feeders. All are migratory, but most of ours don't go far. The ruby-throated and the rufous hummingbirds are notable exceptions, each traveling at least 2,000 miles.

Hummingbirds build cup-like nests of great beauty and delicacy, often covered with lichens and held together with the silk of spider webs. They're lined with plant down, feathers, or fur. About an inch deep and an inch in diameter, from a distance they could be mistaken for a knot or a gall on a tree. After mating, the male leaves for other adventures and the female builds the nest, incubates the two pea-sized eggs, and cares for the nestlings. They're fed at first by regurgitation, as often as five times an hour. The placing of that needle-bill into the nestling's gape has been likened to a surgical procedure.

Hummingbirds spend the time left over from feeding and reproducing in quarreling—with each other (assuming two birds of the same sex) or anybody else that comes along. They're unimpressed by size as a deterring factor and are just as willing to tangle with such enemies as crows, kingbirds, and hawks as with one of their own species. They can escape most enemies because of their superior maneuvering abilities and because they're capable of traveling sixty miles per hour, the speed of a hawk. Though many of the species of hummingbirds live in equatorial jungles, they may also be found in forests, gardens, deserts, plains, canyons, or mountains.

FOND OF FLOWERS

How do you attract these fascinating birds to your garden? With flowers, primarily. Use feeders, by all means, but not feeders alone. Someone gave one of our friends a hummingbird feeder because his patio was practically swarming with hummers. He swears that since he installed it his only visitors have been doves. It's my conviction that feeders are second in importance only to a supply of *natural* food. That means lots of flowers, which can only be considered an additional ornament to your property.

Experimental studies have convinced researchers that hummingbirds are first attracted to red flowers, but contrast is important. Next on their preferred list is white, followed by violet, orange, blue, yellow, and green. It has been suggested that green may be more attractive to them in arid country than it is in more humid areas.

FAVORITES

Some flowers seem almost irresistible to hummingbirds. Particularly recommended are hibiscus, petunias, mimosa, azaleas, trumpet vine, lupines, tree tobacco, salvia, larkspur, flowering quince, monarda (bee balm), ajuga, buckeye, chinaberry, impatiens, zinnias, columbines, snapdragons, dahlias, gladiolas, and fuchsia. Flowers, particularly brilliant ones, attract hummingbirds. Who could ask for a better combination?

Now just a bit of more specific information about some of the hummingbirds you might expect to see. From a line extending through North Dakota and eastern Kansas south to eastern Texas, the area stretching to the Atlantic and Gulf Coasts is unlikely to host any but ruby-throated hummingbirds. In our garden, we usually see the first ones of the season feeding on the flowering quince. Quarrelsome little birds, 3 to 3¾ inches, they mutter irritably to themselves most of the time between sips. In addition to nectar, they ingest small insects and sometimes snack on maple or other sap seeping from bark punctured by sapsuckers.

BLACK-CHINNED HUMMINGBIRD

The black-chinned hummingbird is a close relative of the ruby-throated (the females are virtually indistinguishable in the field) but is found only during migration in any of the same range. The black-chinned lives in semi-arid country, chiefly from western Montana south to central Texas. It sometimes waits on a perch for flying insects, which it pursues in much the same way a flycatcher does.

RUFOUS HUMMINGBIRD

The rufous hummingbird is found as far north as Alaska, east to western Montana and south to central California. He is a veritable tiger among hummingbirds; considering their generally aggressive natures, that's saying a lot. He's especially attracted to red flowers, but he likes sap too. He catches insects from the air and also plucks them from plants and flowers.

The broad-tailed hummingbird is found primarily in foothills and mountains from eastern California through the Rocky Mountains. A regular visitor to gardens and feeders in his range, the broad-tailed is good-sized for a hummingbird on this continent, about 4 to 4½ inches. Costa's hummingbird is a small species, resident in deserts from south central California to southwestern New Mexico. Expect to find him in areas of sagebrush, greasewood, and eucalyptus.

CALLIOPE

The smallest hummingbird usually found in the United States is the calliope, measuring 2¾ to 3½ inches. This mountain resident, which weighs a *tenth* of an ounce, breeds in the Cascades, Sierras, and Rockies.

Other hummingbirds found in the United States in very limited ranges include Rivoli's hummingbird (at five inches, his only rival in size in our country is the blue-throated hummingbird), the buff-bellied, violet-crowned, white-eared, and Lucifer hummingbirds. It is especially difficult to distinguish, in the field, female and juvenile hummingbirds of different species.

ALLEN'S HUMMINGBIRD

Two others of limited range deserve special attention because they're familiar to so many people who stock feeders for them. Allen's hummingbird is similar to the rufous hummingbird, to which he is closely related. He's found only along the Pacific coast from southern Oregon to the Los Angeles area during the breeding season. Insects and nectar comprise his diet. Anna's hummingbird breeds in California and is larger than other hummers found there. Eucalyptus, orange, and red-flowering gooseberry blossoms are among the favorite nectar sources for Anna's hummingbird, which is as common in urban areas as in canyons.

Hummingbirds are, with depressing regularity, described as the (a) jewels or (b) gems of American bird life. That's obviously because of their size and strikingly beautiful plumage. (My quarrel lies with the expression of the sentiment, not with its basis.) Other national treasures, fortunately, are within the scope of our discussion. Every area has a plentiful supply of beautiful and interesting visitors to its feeders.

10
Branching
Out

To conclude, I'd like to mention briefly some specialized categories of birds: game birds, water birds, and birds of prey. There's a bit of overlapping here. Some water birds are considered game birds (ducks and geese, for instance). We've faced similar situations: whether a given dove is a game bird or a songbird often depends on where it lives. For the sake of simplicity, therefore, we'll start with game birds that live on land and are willing to visit feeding stations in selected locations.

GAME BIRDS

Selected locations is the key phrase for game birds (for all the birds in this chapter, in fact). Urban bird feeders aren't likely to see quail or pheasants. Suburban dwellers frequently can manage to attract these birds, but shouldn't expect grouse. Rural bird lovers may get grouse but can't expect to see the reclusive turkeys regularly (though we hear them in the woodlot often enough). All of these birds belong to the order *Galliformes* and are considered chicken-like birds. They live mostly on the ground and are primarily eaters of plant foods. They have strong legs and feet with which to scratch for food. They seldom migrate. Their young are able to run about as soon as they're hatched. The domestic chicken, to name the single most valuable bird, is a member of this order, and so is the turkey. In fact, the domestic turkey is the very same species as the wild one.

We'll begin with quail, members of the family *Phasianidae*, which is found nearly all over the world and also includes pheasants, partridges, and peacocks. Probably the best known quail is the bobwhite, found naturally from the Rockies east to the Atlantic, except in the extreme Northeast. It has been introduced to the Pacific Northwest, Idaho, Hawaii, and west Texas. It's the smallest of our native quail except for the Harlequin quail, found only in a limited range. The bobwhite is inconspicuous looking, but a friendly sort. When there still remained vacant lots around my parents' home in central Florida, they hosted a visiting bevy of quail several times each day. In season, the bobwhites were followed by their young. Mum and Dad's Scottie, Patti, loved to watch them. On several occasions, a juvenile bird detached itself from the flock to investigate Patti carefully. The dog always endured this examination courteously, permitting the little one to rejoin the others in peace.

HOW TO ATTRACT THEM

How do you attract these amiable birds to your yard? Their preferred habitat is brush. They eat seeds and some insects, such as beetles, crickets, and spiders. They'll eat grain you scatter, especially oats and cracked corn. Plants that attract them include sand cherry, redbud, bittersweet, white ash, American beauty berry, American beech, blackberries, vetch, clover, lespedeza, alfalfa, mulberries, amaranth, four o'clocks, and locust.

Gambel's quail, a bird of the Southwest, is also called the desert quail. It is a stunningly beautiful bird, a little larger than the bobwhite, with a black plume extending forward from the crown of its head. Strange and wonderful, reminiscent of the exotic appeal of the peacock. In California, Oregon, and Nevada is found a similar bird, the California quail. Both of these species are able to go without water if sufficient succulent vegetation is available. They eat insects as well as grains, fruits, and berries.

In mountainous areas of Washington, Idaho, Oregon, Nevada, and California you'll find another plumed quail, the mountain quail, also called the plumed partridge. His plume stands straight up. Mountain quail eat fewer insects than other quail, subsisting mostly on grains, seeds, and fruits. The scaled quail, found in eastern Arizona and Colorado east to Kansas and south to the lower Rio Grande Valley, is a bird of arid country. His nickname, "cotton top," refers to his brushy white crest. There's a larger percentage of insects in his diet than in that of any other American quail, and if the vegetation is succulent enough it can supply much of his water requirements.

PHEASANTS

Three introduced birds round out this family. The first of these is the ring-necked pheasant, a large and handsome bird native to Asia. It has successfully adapted, especially to grain farming areas, but is not found in the South or Texas. Many states stock pheasants for hunting. If these birds visit your property, they'll readily accept cracked corn, and they appreciate a supply of grit when there is snow cover. They may wander into your garden for asparagus seeds, and they like dandelions and chokecherries. They're often seen foraging in fields for waste grain. Usually, a cock supervises a number of hens.

The gray or Hungarian partridge is much smaller—twelve to fourteen inches as compared to the thirty to thirty-six inches of a male ring-necked pheasant. It has adapted to the Midwest, Northwest, and prairie states, where it often raids vegetable gardens and grain fields for barley, corn, and buckwheat. It also eats ragweed, ants, and grasshoppers. The chukar partridge, introduced into the western states, feeds on grass, seeds, and insects but visits cultivated fields as well.

PRAIRIE CHICKEN

And that brings us back to native birds, the *Tetraonidae* family of grouse and ptarmigan. The greater prairie chicken, found on the prairies from Canada to Texas, will visit grain fields near buildings but not necessarily your feeding station. The grouse, often popularly called partridges, are northern birds which tend to be shy near settled areas. The ruffed grouse, found coast to coast in the North, is fond of goldenrod, clover, apples, cottonwood, birch, alder, blueberries, high bush cranberries, dandelions, hazelnuts, chokecherries, and Japanese barberry. Norman Wight, an avid birder in Maine, scatters scratch feed for them in the pine trees near his barn. He feeds them apples too, fastened to a stick with nails. Sometimes grouse visit a yard for oats.

ruffed grouse

The sharp-tailed grouse, native to parts of Oregon, Utah, New Mexico, and Nebraska, is unlikely to come to your feeding station but may appear on your land if you grow aspen, birch, oaks, or cranberries. The spruce grouse, found in northern coniferous forests, is extremely limited in range in our country. Don't count on grouse of any kind in your yard. It's quite an accomplishment to entice them, and locale is extremely important.

WATER BIRDS

Some of the water birds are a little easier—a mixed blessing, maybe, but easier. Gulls, for example, especially the ring-billed and Bonaparte's (order *Charadriiformes*, family *Laridae*) think bread and potato chips are wonderful, but if you want to try something more substantial, they get a little fussy. Meat or fish scraps, fine, but forget about the birdseed. People whose houses have tiled roofs sometimes curse gulls who have learned that a roof is a dandy place for dropping shells to open them. Unfortunately, the shells tend also to open tile roofs.

You don't live where there are gulls? Almost any city park with a body of water in it has geese and ducks, wild and domestic,

gull

which are as hungry for handouts as any pigeon. Mallards (ancestors of most domestic ducks) and Canada geese are found all over the country. They are all members of the order *Anseriformes*, family *Anatidae*. They range from medium-sized to large, and all of them have webbed feet and bills with sawtooth edges.

CAN BE PROBLEMS

Sometimes, when these geese and ducks find a likely looking place, they decide to forget all about migration. In their enthu-

Canada geese

siasm to provide suitable habitat for geese, some cities and towns—some states, even—have managed to create king-sized problems for themselves. You think pigeon droppings are a nuisance? Geese are much worse. The birds become half-tame very willingly if ample food is available. Some people, and some agencies of government, plant grain for the visitors. But geese can't—and don't—discriminate between what's planted for them and what's planted for market. They're big birds with enormous appetites. A flock of them can strip a field in short order. Gleaning is one thing, and many farmers welcome migrants stopping for a snack, *after* the harvest. But what has happened in some areas is that geese, both imported and migrant, have found the living so fine they've settled in permanently. They raise families, which in turn—but you see how it goes. The grain fields of farmers begin to suffer.

The same thing can happen on a small scale—to you. Having raised domestic geese and ducks, I'm painfully aware of the extent of their appetites. We don't feed the wild ones. We're glad a pair of mallards nests at the brook behind the back pasture. We're delighted to see the Canada geese stopping in the cornfield next to us on their way south. I know of no avian event more exciting than the migration of geese. At the first honk, I drop whatever I'm doing and rush outdoors to watch until they're out of sight and hearing. What splendid creatures they are! However dreary the day, seeing them exhilarates me. But they're going to have to hustle for themselves. Enough is enough.

Of course it's up to you. With bread and corn, it's possible to attract Canada geese, mallards, ring-necked ducks, and the lesser scaup, all of them common over most of the United States. Just remember that some municipalities have had so much success in such efforts that now they're "transplanting" Canada geese.

SWANS

Swans belong in the same family with ducks and geese, but you're not likely to observe native swans at close range. Just seeing them passing aloft is a rare treat for most of us. Our native swans are the trumpeter (which at thirty pounds and measuring up to seventy-two inches is the largest swan) and the whistling swans. Trumpeter swans are increasing in numbers, but the whistling swan is our only relatively common swan. It winters usually from Chesapeake Bay to North Carolina and from southern Alaska to southern California, with some found in the Great Basin, the Lower Colorado River, and New Mexico. In other areas it is chiefly a migrant.

The mute swan (an introduced species established along the Middle Atlantic coast as a resident), found frequently as a more or less domestic ornament to ponds and rivers, measures sixty inches. It is the one that most of us are likely to see. Swans, especially during the nesting season, have notoriously short fuses, so be careful. A blow from those powerful wings is no joke, and they're proficient in the use of their beaks as weapons. Nesting swans sometimes attack and kill birds (ducks, for instance) which inadvertently venture too near their nests.

You can branch out to the gallinules and coots, order *Gruiformes*, family *Rallidae*. Coots become quite bold about asking for bread and grain. You think jays and grosbeaks are voracious? Wait until you see how the water birds can eat. The only birds I've encountered that can top them in terms of sheer volume consumed are the emus and ostriches that gather around the cars going through the safari-type game parks.

BIRDS OF PREY

There's a final major group of birds that ought to be mentioned, though they aren't feeder birds: the birds of prey. Predators are traditionally a contingent we take care to bar from the feeder; birds of prey have had rabid enemies among people who maintain feeding stations.

Birds of prey include both day- and night-flying raptors. That word "raptor" means *any* bird of prey, and I use it to avoid offending birders who, quite rightly, wince when they hear all day-flying raptors lumped together as hawks. Not all birds of prey belong to the same order, let alone the same family. Owls belong to the order *Strigiformes*. Falcons, accipiters, buteos, eagles, and vultures are found in the order *Falconiformes*. And there is one other order, *Passeriformes*, that contains a predatory family, the shrikes. This last order, you'll remember, is the order of perching birds, which contains also the great bulk of our feeder birds.

If you maintain a feeding station, you'll occasionally see song-birds taken by birds of prey. No need to get agitated. There was a time when misinformed bird lovers felt obliged to wage war on birds of prey. No question about it, it's a shock to the average bird-lover's nervous system to see a Cooper's hawk strike a robin on the lawn. We have to remember that all these birds that sometimes prey on songbirds prey also on rodents. They're a positive boon to agriculture. If that's still not good enough to help you to accept the situation, remind yourself that it's no "worse" than to see that same charming robin dining on a grasshopper. We tend to become upset about the whole business whenever the animal food of some creature we admire happens to be one of the higher animals, but it's not a reasonable attitude. Bear in mind that there are relatively few vegetarians among human beings.

I'm not suggesting that you'll want to *provide* dinner for birds of prey. Occasionally an injured one will visit your feeder. Occasionally you may see a hunter surveying the situation. The former is no menace, and the latter isn't likely to capture any but diseased or injured birds. You may discover that the heightened appreciation of songbirds that accompanies having a feeder in your yard will gradually grow into an interest in other kinds of birds.

And that's what it's all about. It's easy to admire deer and foxes and raccoons, but maybe you'll eventually acquire a certain fondness for porcupines and moles and skunks. Who knows? In time, you may find that even reptiles and amphibians have a lot going for them. From that point, it's only a short step to respect for wasps and woolly worms. Viewed without prejudice, the natural world is downright fascinating. Enjoy. Throw out a crust. Invite the birds to dinner.

A
Selected
Annotated
Bibliography

A trip to the library or bookstore will indicate the tremendous amount of material available on birds. The books I've listed here don't even come close to exhausting the subject. They're merely a sampling of the kinds of things you'll encounter and were selected to give you a general idea of what to expect. You can be reasonably sure of finding something to your tastes, whatever your particular area of interest. Periodicals are another source of information. Anyone who's enthusiastic about birds will want to look at *Audubon* regularly. It will guide you to still other sources and is especially useful to make you aware of new material.

Bagg, Aaron C. and Eliot, Samuel A., Jr. *Birds of the Connecticut Valley in Massachusetts.* Northampton, MA: Hampshire Bookshop, 1937. Wherever you live, you'll be able to find a reference work as specialized for your region as this one is for its area. Remember, however, that times change. The date of publication will, in many cases, dictate a point of view. In addition, it must limit the content because more information becomes available and changes occur in range and/or habitat.

Baynes, Ernest Harold. *Wild Bird Guests.* New York: E. P. Dutton, 1915. Baynes writes with great affection for certain species. For those with which he's not in sympathy he advocates death: shoot 'em, poison 'em, trap 'em.

Blachly, Lou and Jenks, Randolph. *Naming the Birds at a Glance.* New York: Alfred A. Knopf, 1970. A reference book, to be used instead of, or in conjunction with, a field guide.

Burtt, Harold E. *The Psychology of Birds: An Interpretation of Bird Behavior.* New York: The MacMillan Company, 1967. Interesting, informative. Not to be confused with light reading.

Collins, Henry Hill, Jr. *Complete Field Guide to American Wildlife.* New York: Harper & Row, Publishers, 1959. Not just birds, of course, but the bird section is useful, particularly because of the distribution maps.

Collins, Henry H., Jr. and Boyajian, Ned R. *Familar Garden Birds of America.* New York: Harper & Row, Publishers, 1965. Highly recommended as a useful adjunct to a field guide, this one goes into nesting habits and other behavior.

Darling, Lois and Louis. *Bird.* Boston: Houghton Mifflin, 1962. A model of clarity on birds, generalized. If you're interested in bird anatomy and physiology, this book provides a good introduction to the subject.

Davison, Verne E. *Attracting Birds: from the Prairies to the Atlantic.* New York: Thomas Y. Crowell Company, 1967. Exhaustive study of the food preferences of birds. Not to be confused with entertainment.

Dennis, John V. *Beyond the Bird Feeder.* New York: Alfred A. Knopf, 1981. Interesting bird behavior: what they're up to when they're not partaking of delicacies you provide.

Fisher, James. *A History of Birds.* Boston: Houghton Mifflin, 1954. Straightforward. (Yawn.)

Fisher, James. *Watching Birds.* London: Penguin Books, 1951. General, worldwide.

Forbush, E. H. *Birds of Massachusetts and Other New England States.* 3 volumes. Boston: Commonwealth of Massachusetts, 1925–29. Limited to a region, yes, but a region that has many birds common to the entire country. One of the classics.

Govan, Ada Clapham. *Wings at My Window.* New York: The MacMillan Company, 1942. Once considered sweet and inspiring. The gentle lady championed shooting hawks and frightening jays and starlings out of their wits.

Hanzák, J. *The Pictorial Encyclopedia of Birds.* London: Paul Hamlyn, 1967. Just what you'd expect, with fine plates.

Howard, Len. *Birds as Individuals.* New York: Doubleday, 1953. Interesting, but decidedly weird. Ms. Howard literally invites the birds in. Into the house. English.

Kress, Stephen W. *The Audubon Society Handbook for Birders*. New York: Charles Scribner's Sons, 1981. Check it thoroughly if you plan to go birding beyond your garden.

Laycock, George. *The Bird Watcher's Bible*. Garden City, New York: Doubleday & Co., Inc., 1976. General in scope, with useful sections on bird banding, binoculars, cameras, and bird photography.

Martin, Alfred G. *Hand-Taming Wild Birds at the Feeder*. Freeport, Maine: Bond Wheelwright, 1967. You want chickadees to eat from your hand? Here's how to go about training them.

McClung, Robert M. *America's Endangered Birds*. New York: William Morrow and Company, 1979. Who's got problems and what's being done about them.

McElroy, Thomas P. *The Habitat Guide to Birding*. New York: Alfred A. Knopf, 1974. Excellent for what to expect and where.

McKenny, Margaret. *Birds in the Garden: And How to Attract Them*. New York: Grosset & Dunlap, Publishers, 1939. Has most of the indefensible characteristics of its period, but the garden sections are useful. Dull, too.

Millar, Margaret. *The Birds and the Beasts Were There*. New York: Random House, 1967. Highly recommended, a first-rate book. In terms of usefulness, it's particularly geared to the West, specifically the Santa Barbara area. But hang geography, it's splendid reading.

Murphy, Robert Cushman and Amadon, Dean. *Land Birds of America*. New York: McGraw Hill Book Company, Inc., 1953. Beautiful illustrations. Recommended.

Pearson, T. Gilbert. *Birds of America*. Garden City, New York: Garden City Publishing Company, Inc., 1936. Another classic. Keep the date in mind, but aside from its necessary limitations, a most useful— and charming—book.

Peterson, Alvin M. *The ABC of Attracting Birds*. New York: The Bruce Publishing Company, 1937. Forget it.

Peterson, Roger Tory. *The Birds*. New York: Time, Inc., 1963. Worldwide. Fascinating. Excellent plates.

Peterson, Roger Tory. *A Field Guide to the Birds*. Boston: Houghton Mifflin, 1947. The standard field guide for east of the Rockies.

Peterson, Roger Tory. *A Field Guide to Western Birds*. Second edition. Boston: Houghton Mifflin Company, 1961. Ditto for the Rockies to the Pacific. You'll probably want to own one or the other. Or both.

Pettingill, Olin Sewall, Jr. *A Guide to Bird Finding: East of the Mississippi.* Second edition. Boston: Houghton Mifflin Co., 1977. There's a western version of this one too. If you're going birding, this is valuable. Parks, sanctuaries, refuges, and what you can expect to find therein are listed state by state.

Pough, Richard H. *Audubon Bird Guide: Small Land Birds of Eastern and Central North America from Southern Texas to Central Greenland.* New York: Doubleday & Co., Inc., 1946. Excellent. More complete information than the usual field guide, but it could be used as one. No game birds or day-flying raptors. See also *Audubon Western Bird Guide* (1957).

Rand, Austin L. *American Water and Game Birds.* New York: E. P. Dutton & Company, Inc., 1956. Interesting with excellent plates.

Robbins, Chandler S., Brunn, Bertel and Zim, Herbert S. *Birds of North America.* New York: Golden Press, 1966. North of Mexico, that is. Excellent.

Rome, Claire. *An Owl Came to Stay.* New York: Crown Publishers, Inc., 1979. So-so.

Scheithauer, Walter. *Hummingbirds.* New York: Thomas Y. Crowell, 1967. Another example of the specialized books available.

Schutz, Walter E. *Bird Watching, Housing and Feeding.* Milwaukee: The Bruce Publishing Company, 1963. Revised edition entitled *How to Attract, House and Feed Birds.* New York: Bruce, 1970. Recommended for birdhouse plans.

Staples, C. Percival. *Birds in a Garden Sanctuary.* London: Frederick Warne & Co., Ltd., 1946. Interesting and many applications to the United States, but it *is* about British birds and gardens.

Stefferud, Alfred, Editor. *Birds in Our Lives.* Washington, D. C.: U.S. Dept. of the Interior, 1966. Many articles on a host of subjects, including the economic impact of birds.

Terres, John K. *The Audubon Society Encyclopedia of North American Birds.* New York: Alfred A. Knopf, 1980. It's—well—encyclopedic. Impressive. Wildly expensive, too. Strictly a reference book.

Terres, John K. *Songbirds in Your Garden.* New York: Thomas Y. Crowell, 1968. For the general reader, this one is more interesting than the *Encyclopedia.*

Tucker, James A. *Florida Birds.* Tampa: Lewis A. Maxwell, 1968. Still another example of the useful sort of handbook available for limited areas.

Wetmore, Alexander. *Song and Garden Birds of North America.* Washington, D. C.: National Geographic Society, 1964. Stunningly beautiful book and one worth reading, too. National Geographic also publishes one on water and game birds.

Index